MEDICAL
+ CORPS +
HEROES OF
WORLD WAR II

MEDICAL +CORPS+ HEROES OF WORLD WAR II

★ ★ ★ ★ ★ ★ ★ ★ ★ ★ ★ ★ ★

by Wyatt Blassingame

PURPLE HOUSE PRESS
Kentucky

Look for *Combat Nurses of World War II*
by Wyatt Blassingame from Purple House Press

For permission to quote from unpublished letters, the author is grateful to Dr. John S. Ewing, Vernon Floyd, Dr. Parker C. Hardin, Dr. G. Mason Kahn, Bentz Plagemann, and Sam C. Schiek.

Front cover: Army medics work hard to get this litter case over the difficult terrain on Okinawa to an aid station. April 20, 1945
Back cover: In an underground surgery room, behind the front lines on Bougainville, an American Army doctor operates on a U.S. soldier wounded by a Japanese sniper. Papua New Guinea, December 13, 1943
Page 2: In a gully, Navy doctors and corpsmen administer plasma to wounded Marines at an aid station on Iwo Jima. February 20, 1945
Page 5: Medic on duty with soldiers awaiting firing orders in a dugout in Ubach, Germany. January 7, 1945
Page 170-171: Wounded men from the *Nevada* are transferred to an amphibious craft for further transfer to a Navy hospital ship. Okinawa, July 17, 1945

Photo credits:
U.S. Army: pages 6, 99, 110, 166
U.S. Coast Guard: page 106 top, 106 bottom
U.S. Department of Defense: page 76 top
U.S. Marine Corps Archives: pages 18, 36, 71, 159
U.S. Navy: pages 11 top, 11 bottom, 57, 84, 132, 135, 170-171
Library of Congress: pages 27, 60 top, 60 bottom, 65
Ministry of Defence UK: page 104
National Archives: front cover, back cover, pages 2, 5, 33, 43, 50, 76 bottom, 81, 97, 109, 116, 123, 141, 146, 152, 164
National Library of Medicine: pages 89 top, 89 bottom, 93, 94, 113 top, 113 bottom,
National Museum of Health and Medicine: page 126
Naval Heritage and History: page 149

Published by
Purple House Press
PO Box 787
Cynthiana, Kentucky 41031

Classic Books for Kids and Young Adults
purplehousepress.com

Copyright © 1969 by Wyatt Blassingame. Printed with permission from the estate of Wyatt Blassingame
"About the Author" copyright © 2021 by Kathi Diamant
Cover design and photo arrangement © 2022 by Purple House Press
Revised edition. All rights reserved.

ISBN 9781948959674 Hardcover
ISBN 9781948959681 Paperback

CONTENTS

1. Pearl Harbor, Wake, and the Philippines — 7
2. Training for the Medical Corps — 26
3. Guadalcanal — 34
4. The Loss of a Portable Hospital — 58
5. Solomons, Gilberts, and other Pacific Islands — 67
6. The Beachhead at Anzio — 82
7. D-Day — 96
8. Germany's Western Front — 108
9. Army and Navy Medics at Sea — 124
10. Iwo Jima and Okinawa — 144
    Author's Note — 167
    About the Author — 168
    Pacific Theater map — 16

A fireboat pours water onto the burning battleship *West Virginia* in Pearl Harbor, on December 7, 1941.

PEARL HARBOR, WAKE, AND THE PHILIPPINES
CHAPTER ONE

It was Sunday morning and there were few patients in the sick bay of the old battleship *Nevada*. Ned Curtis, Pharmacist's Mate 2nd Class, had the duty. He was supposed to report at 0800 (8 a.m.), but following the Navy's custom, he came in fifteen minutes early. He went over the lists with the hospital corpsmen going off duty, checked the date—it was December 7, 1941—and said formally, "You are relieved." Then, because there wasn't any work to be done at the moment, he wandered over to look out the porthole.

Pearl Harbor lay placid under the blue Hawaiian sky. A hundred yards away a garbage lighter was moving toward the *Nevada*, pushing a bow wave of scummy, oil-stained water. Beyond that a motor launch was taking off-duty sailors ashore. And from somewhere—it sounded as if it might be back toward Ford Island—came a dull series of jarring thumps. Ned Curtis wondered what kind of work was going on over there on Sunday morning.

Suddenly there was another thump, louder, closer, an explosion of some kind. And all at once the *Nevada's* sick bay jarred to the clash and clang of the call to battle stations.

Several of the off-duty corpsmen had been sleeping in sick bay. This was carrying things too far, some of the men felt, to have an air-raid drill on Sunday morning! But nevertheless they grabbed their clothes on the run. And then over the public-address system came an excited voice crying, "This is no drill! We are being bombed by Jap aircraft!"

Ned Curtis' battle station was in sick bay, so he just stood where he was, feeling dazed. Overhead the *Nevada's* guns were firing now. He could feel the vibrations. He saw the last of the patients who had been in sick bay run in a small, frantic circle looking for clothes that weren't there, then dash for his battle station still wearing pajamas. The sick bay was empty now, except for the other corpsmen and the doctor whose stations were here. One of the corpsmen was saying, "I still think it's a drill. I still think…"

The ship leaped. Curtis was thrown into the air and came down rolling. When he was standing again he heard one of the other corpsmen saying, "…torpedo hit us somewhere forward."

After that the first casualties began to arrive. As they did the ship shuddered and lunged again, struck topside by bombs. Moments later the call came down from the forward antiaircraft fire director, high up on the foremast. "Ensign Taussig has been hit. He needs help."

It occurred to Curtis that this was not the way it was supposed to be done in a drill. The injured man should be given first aid, then taken to sick bay or a battle dressing station. But this was no drill. "I'll go," he said without waiting for orders, and was running, his first-aid pouch in his hand.

He had to cross the open deck. All around him guns were firing, a shuddering world of noise. A hundred yards away the *Arizona* was a mass of smoke and flame from which one explosion followed another. As Curtis ran something leaped from the deck ahead of him; there were thin, screeching sounds beneath the boom of the guns. Machine-gun bullets, he thought; we're being strafed. Then he was climbing steel ladders up the foremast.

Here Ensign Joe Taussig lay on his back with two sailors kneeling over him. One leg of Taussig's trousers had been ripped away, exposing a gaping wound at the thigh. The ensign was trying to hold the lips of the wound together with his fingers, but the blood was running freely over his hand onto the deck.

I've got to move fast, Ned Curtis thought, but I've got to do it right. He forced his hands to be steady. He sprinkled sulfa on Taussig's wound and put on a battle dressing. He was about to give the ensign a shot of morphine when Taussig said, "Wait."

Another bomb hit the *Nevada*. Flame-filled smoke shot skyward. The flame did not touch the men in the small cubicle high above the deck, but the smoke and the heat did. The deck on which they stood was becoming unbearably hot.

"Wait," Taussig said again. He rolled his head, looking around him. "You can't get me down from here. And you can't stay here. Go below, all of you."

"We'll get you down," Curtis said, and jabbed the needle into the ensign.

"Leave me and go below. That's an order."

Nobody seemed to hear him. One of the sailors said, "The ship's under way!"

Looking up Curtis saw that the *Nevada* was moving. But she was going to pass very close to the blazing *Arizona*. Already smoke was rolling into the fire director in an almost solid mass. "Here," Curtis said. He dipped cotton into water and passed the pieces to the other sailors. "Hold it over your nose and mouth. It'll filter some of the smoke."

He was about to put wet cotton over Taussig's mouth when the ensign said, "You can't save me; but if you stay here you'll all die."

With terrible slowness the *Nevada* moved through the *Arizona's* smoke. It was the only battleship that managed to leave its anchorage in an effort to fight clear. And like brown hawks Japanese planes swooped on it, guns blazing, bombs hurtling down. Near misses sent great geysers of water leaping into the air close alongside. Then there was a direct hit, perhaps two of them. New fires blazed up to increase the already unbearable heat in the fire director.

At almost the same time that Hospital Corpsman Ned Curtis was kneeling beside Ensign Taussig, Dr. John Moorhead was leaving his hotel on Waikiki Beach a

ABOVE: The *Nevada* on fire after the Japanese attack. "The ship that wouldn't sink" went on to take part in the battles of Attu, Normandy, Southern France, Iwo Jima, and Okinawa.

BELOW: Smoke billowing from the shattered *Arizona*.

few miles away. Moorhead had been an Army doctor during World War I. Later he became a famous New York surgeon. Now he was in Hawaii to give a series of medical lectures. The lecture this morning was to be on "The Treatment of Burns."

Somewhere in the hotel lobby a man's voice shouted, "The Japs are bombing Pearl Harbor!"

The Hawaiian doctor walking alongside Moorhead only laughed. "We hear that kind of wild rumor about once a week," he said. "Those are guns you hear, but it's only the Army having antiaircraft practice."

A few minutes later, driving toward the auditorium where Moorhead was to lecture, the Hawaiian doctor turned on his car radio. "This is no drill," the announcer was saying. "Japanese planes are over Pearl Harbor. Bombs…"

The two doctors listened in a daze. They were both civilians. They drove on to the auditorium because they didn't know what else to do.

There were about fifty doctors at the auditorium. Dr. Moorhead was ready to begin his lecture when another doctor rushed in. "The Army wants twelve surgeons!" he shouted. "Right away at Tripler Hospital. Who'll go?"

In one surge all the doctors bolted from the room.

To Dr. John Moorhead what followed was a kind of blur. There was the wild ride through crowded streets. Ahead of them great clouds of smoke and flame towered into the sky. The Japanese planes were gone now but explosions continued as burning ships and planes blew apart.

Then Moorhead was in the hospital, scrubbed down faster than he had ever scrubbed before, and operating on the wounded. There were men with an arm gone, or a leg. Men ripped open by shrapnel. And burned. He had never seen so many burn cases. And I was about to lecture on the treatment of burns, he thought.

High above the deck of the *Nevada* Ned Curtis gave silent thanks to the Navy's foresight. There was a stretcher within reach. Curtis wrapped Ensign Taussig in a blanket to protect him from the heat and strapped him to the stretcher. One end of the stretcher was fastened to a line.

"You fellows lower him," Curtis said. "I'll go with him to keep the stretcher from fouling on the mast."

He began the slow descent of the steel ladders. They were almost red hot now. Curtis had wrapped his hands in bandages, but they gave only slight protection when time and again he had to stop to swing the stretcher free of some protruding beam. Below him smoke and flame boiled in half a dozen places. But eventually the stretcher reached the main deck.

Then the men who had lowered Taussig came down.

The *Nevada* was in the channel now, heavily damaged and almost out of control. If she sank in the channel she might block a good part of what remained of the U.S. fleet. To prevent this, two tugs came alongside. They helped fight the fires and at the same time pushed the slowly sinking ship out of the channel and onto the beach at Waipio Point.

Ned Curtis did not see this. Severely burned, he was back at his battle station, working among the wounded and dying.

★

At Tripler Hospital, Dr. John Moorhead worked until he lost track of time. His legs ached. From constant bending over the operating table, his neck felt as though he had been beaten with a baseball bat. But one patient followed another and only when his eyes blurred did the doctor pause to rest.

It was at this point that the hospital commandant stopped by to speak to him. "We are very glad to have you here, Doctor."

"I was in the Army during the first World War," Moorhead told him. "Maybe I ought to go back on active duty." He spoke a little wistfully. He was too old, he thought, for active duty.

It was sometime in the afternoon when the commandant stopped by again. "It's done, Colonel."

"What's done?"

"You're in the Army. A Colonel."

Probably no man was ever taken into the Army faster and with less red tape. Quite possibly it could not have happened to anyone except a famous surgeon. Just how the commandant managed it, Dr. Moorhead never knew, and at this point he had no time even to wonder.

"Thanks," he said, and turned back to the operating table.

★

The International Date Line lies between Hawaii and the tiny island of Wake. When it was Sunday, December 7 in Pearl Harbor, it was Monday, December 8 in Wake. At 0650 (6:50 a.m.) most of the 449 Marines stationed there were at breakfast. Lieutenant (j.g.) Mason Kahn, a young Navy doctor assigned to the Marines, was in the small first-aid tent doing his morning rounds when he heard the bugler sound "Call to Arms."

It was just another drill, Dr. Kahn thought, and kept on with his work. A few minutes later a corpsman rushed into the tent. "It's no drill, Doc! The Japs are bombing Pearl Harbor!"

A few months before, Wake had been nothing more than a tiny atoll where Pan American airplanes refueled on trans-Pacific flights. Then the Navy had sent a thousand civilian workers here to develop a base, along with a small Marine detachment to protect it. The civilians had a doctor of their own named Lawton Shank and a small but fairly well-equipped hospital. The Marines had a first-aid tent and nothing else. Plans had been made, in case of war, to transfer the Marine sick and wounded to the civilian hospital.

"I'd best go see Dr. Shank," Kahn said.

Wake is a narrow V-shaped island with another small island at each tip. The Marine first-aid tent was on the western leg, the civilian hospital on the eastern leg. Dr. Kahn drove over in a truck, and he and Shank made their plans. While they talked a heavy rain squall drifted across the island. A few minutes before noon the rain quit, but

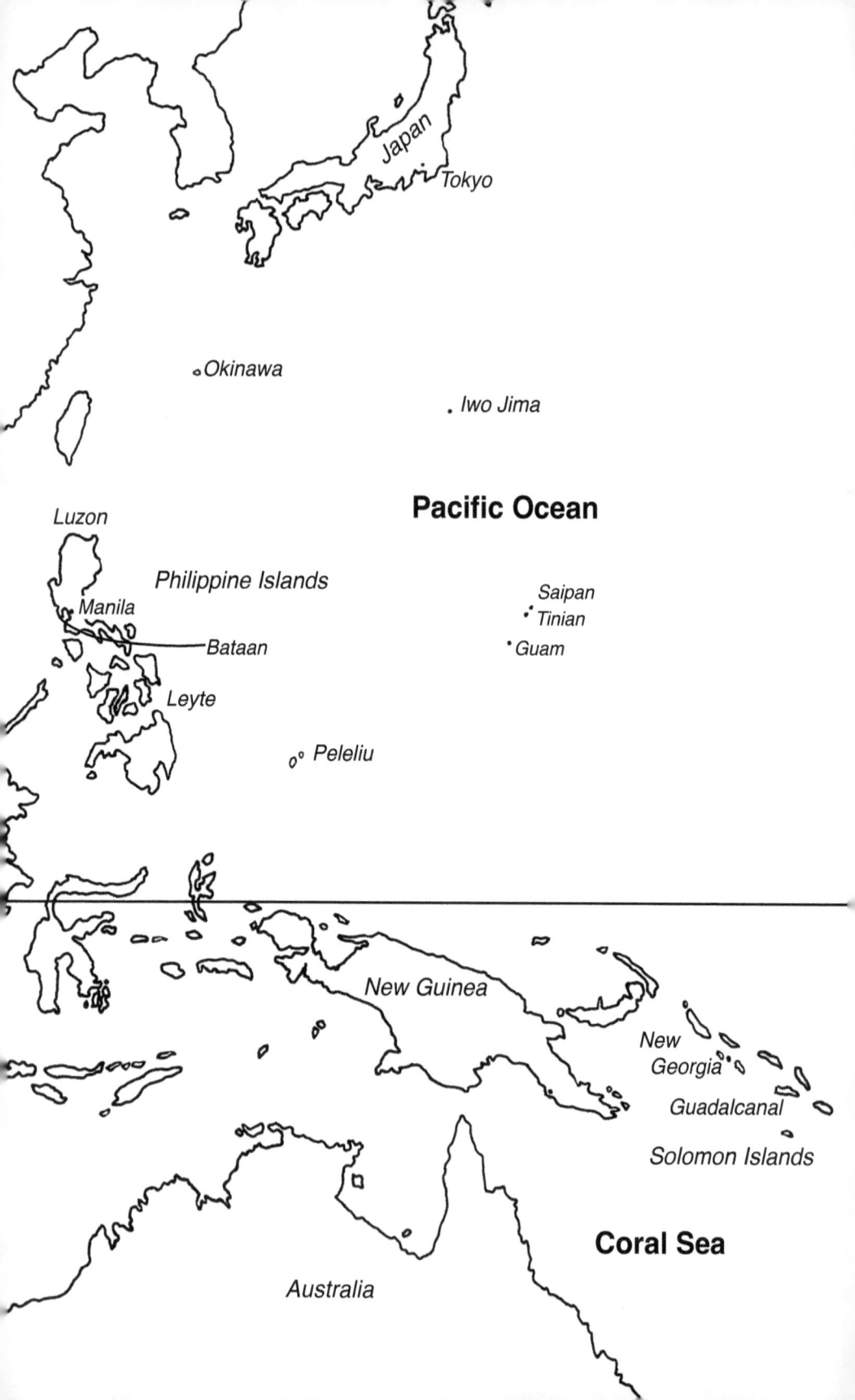

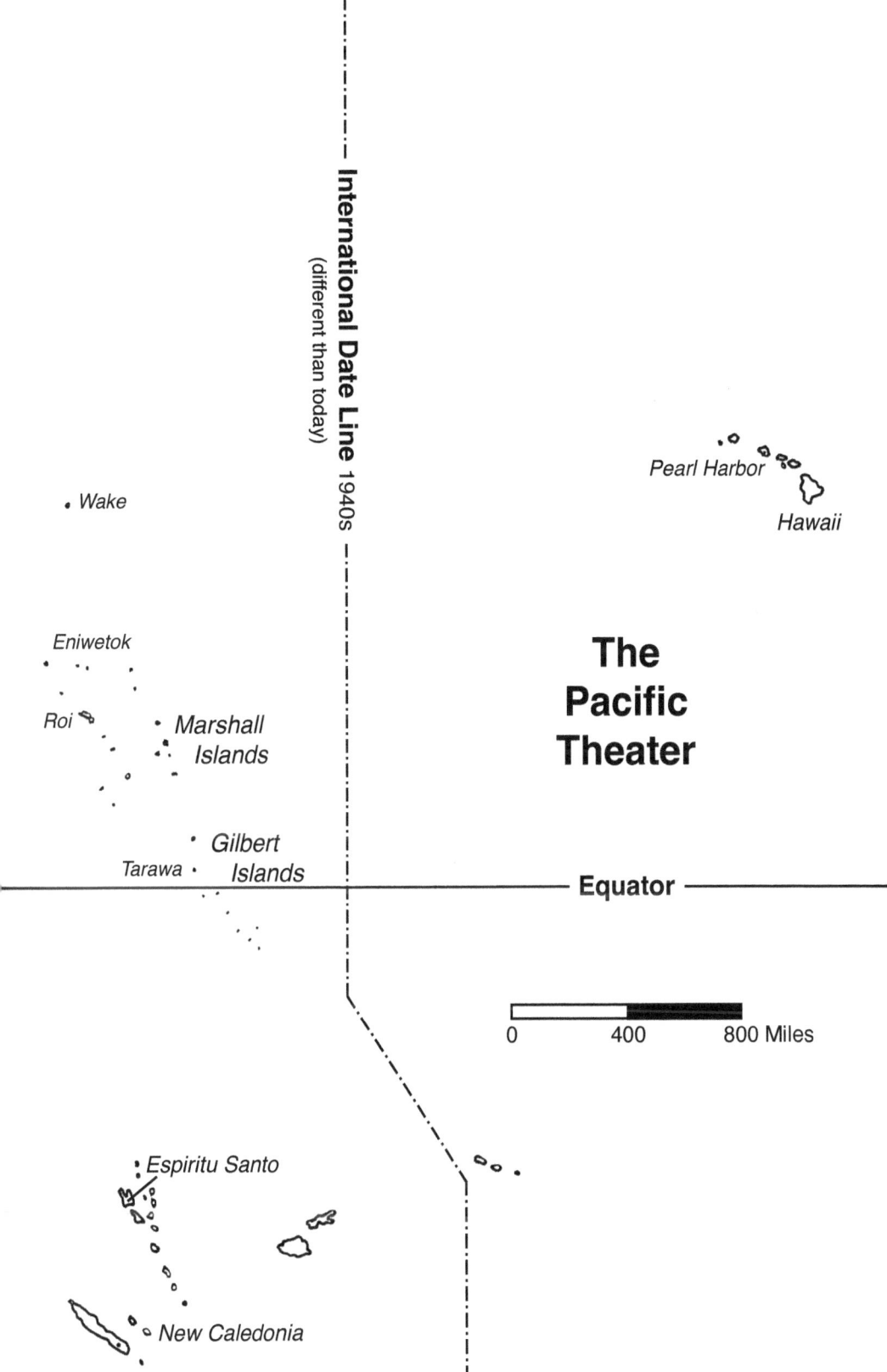

A wounded Marine being helped by a comrade.

there were still thick clouds to the south. Out of these clouds, flying only a few hundred feet high and over the island before they could be seen, came thirty-six Japanese bombers.

They struck the Marine camp Kahn had just left, strafing and bombing. They roared over the small airfield on which were parked eight of the twelve fighter planes stationed there. Then they were gone.

Behind them they left seven of the eight planes afire. Around the planes lay their pilots and mechanics, dead or wounded. Quickly corpsmen brought them to the hospital, along with other Marines and civilians who had been caught in the attack. All afternoon and all night the two doctors worked steadily.

It was daylight when they went to sleep, but they were up again before noon. Everyone knew the distance to Roi, the nearest Japanese base. A bomber taking off from Roi at daybreak would be over Wake about noon.

And at noon the Japanese came. This time the Americans saw them before they reached the island. A gun fired three times fast served as an air-raid warning.

In the hospital, plans had already been made. Patients who could be moved were taken out of their beds and placed on the floor beneath them. Men who could walk hid in closets. When everything was done that could be, Dr. Kahn tossed a heavy trunk onto a cot and crawled underneath it.

Seconds later the Japanese planes roared over the island, bombing and strafing. The hospital began to shake from the impact of bombs nearby. A bullet ripped through the cot above Dr. Kahn, through his trouser leg, and into the floor—without touching him. Then a 100-pound bomb hit the hospital itself.

The floor beneath Dr. Kahn seemed to lift suddenly, throwing him into the air. He came down, rolling, dazed.

Later he could not remember how long it took to get to his feet.

The hospital was a shambles. Men who had been operated on the night before had been killed in their beds. Men with broken legs were crawling across the wrecked floor. The splintered walls were afire. As rapidly as possible doctors and corpsmen dragged the wounded to safety.

With the hospital destroyed, two first-aid stations were set up, one in the charge of Dr. Kahn, the other under Dr. Shank. Both were in concrete bunkers that had been built to house ammunition. Here the wounded men were safe from everything except a direct hit by a heavy bomb.

Major James Devereux, the Marines' commanding officer, ordered the doctors to remain inside their bunkers except for a few minutes in the morning and late afternoon. Devereux knew that if the doctors were killed or injured, it might wreck the morale of his fighting men. And no one knew how long the little island might have to hold out before relief came.

Actually, relief never came to the men on Wake. Too much of the U.S. fleet had been destroyed at Pearl Harbor.

For three days the Japanese bombed the island. On December 11, they tried to land troops. But American shore guns and planes sank two of the Japanese ships, damaged seven others, and beat off the attack.

The Japanese went back to bombing. Each day, promptly at noon, their planes came over. One by one the remaining American fighter planes were destroyed, the antiaircraft guns knocked out. After every raid, corpsmen brought new wounded into the aid stations.

Each morning, and again in the late afternoon, Dr. Kahn went outside the bunker. For a few minutes he would stand on a sand dune looking at the sky, drawing the clean air deep into his lungs. Then he would go back inside to the wounded men.

Shortly after midnight on December 23 the Japanese invaded the island. Now there were no planes left to oppose them. Most of the shore guns had been destroyed. The Japanese fought their way ashore. Little by little they drove back the handful of Marines.

In the hospital bunker Dr. Kahn knew the Japanese were ashore, but he had no way of knowing just how the battle was going. There wasn't even time to wonder. Newly wounded men were coming in, and there was more work to be done. But he could hear the firing as it drew closer and closer.

Finally word came over the field telephone. The island had surrendered. The bunker doors were to be opened and a white flag placed on top, along with a Red Cross emblem. Later Dr. Kahn would write: "We followed instructions. When the Japanese came to the bunker they found not only myself and the corpsmen plus the wounded, but some Marines who had sought sanctuary with us. We were all marched out, stripped of all personal belongings, had all our clothing removed, our hands tied behind our backs with whatever was available. Then we sat on the coral for a period of some hours until the Japanese felt they had secured the island and it was safe to release our bonds."

Ahead of them lay four years of prison.

On the same day that Pearl Harbor and Wake were attacked, the Japanese also hit American bases in the Philippines. Here the fighting went on for five months. On Luzon, the main Philippine island, the American and Filipino troops were pushed into the narrow, jungle-clad peninsula of Bataan. As time went on, disease and starvation became worse enemies than the Japanese. There was little food except rice. The Americans quickly got sick of it, but for awhile they tried to treat it as a joke.

"Oh, boy!" one would say. "Rice! We haven't had this since the last meal!"

"Rice is the best food there is," another would say. "Because anything you do to it helps."

But as the rice gave out, the men quit joking. For awhile the medics working in the hospitals got a little extra food. But as rations grew shorter, everything had to be saved for the patients. The medics lived, like the soldiers in the lines, on what they could get. They ate monkeys and lizards and dug roots in the jungle.

Most of the men had malaria. Many had scurvy, dysentery, beriberi. The Japanese controlled the air. They strafed and bombed anything that moved along the roads, and so ambulances could operate only at night. In the daytime medics worked in the front lines with the soldiers; at night they carried the wounded to the hospitals. Exhausted, weak from starvation and disease, stretcher-bearers often stumbled and fell—and got up and went on again.

The hospitals were converted garages and warehouses. But soon they could not hold all the sick and wounded.

Men were placed on cots under the trees. In the crude operating rooms the doctors worked round the clock. More than once the hospitals were bombed.

Under these conditions heroism became an everyday thing. A soldier being operated on under a local anesthetic heard the roar of diving planes directly overhead.

"Doc," he said, "leave me! Get under a table! Get in a foxhole!"

"If they kill me," the doctor said, "they'll kill me while I'm working." And he kept on.

Pharmacist's Mate Tom Locklear was driving an ambulance when he saw a building that he knew held wounded men being attacked by Japanese planes. He headed for it—and a plane swooped down on his ambulance, shooting it full of holes. A bomb blew the ambulance off the road into a ditch, throwing Locklear out. He got up, bleeding, and climbed back into the ambulance. The steering gear was damaged, but it would still run, swerving wildly from side to side. Locklear drove it to the burning building. He raced inside, brought out the wounded men, and drove them to safety.

After the fall of Bataan, the small island of Corregidor in Manila Bay was the only part of the Philippines left in American hands. Now the Japanese turned their full fury on it. Planes bombed it by day; artillery based on Bataan shelled it day and night. Life on Corregidor, one medic said, was like living on a bullseye.

Tunnels had been dug into several hills on the island

and a hospital was set up in some of these. It was safe in the tunnels. But outside men had to stand watch at the guns and observation posts. And here medics also set up first-aid stations.

Pharmacist's Mate 1st Class Jim Wilson was on duty in the Navy's tunnel when word came on the field telephone that one of the first-aid stations had taken a direct hit. Without a word to anyone Wilson picked up a large box of first-aid supplies and started out of the tunnel.

George Head, another pharmacist's mate, stopped him. "Where are you going?"

"I've got to help those men," Wilson said.

"You can't get to them," Head said. "Listen."

A flight of Japanese planes was overhead and the island shook with the pounding of their bombs. At the same time there was a heavy artillery bombardment from Bataan. "You'll have to wait," Head said.

"They need help now." Wilson went out of the tunnel, and Head went with him. Just outside there was a camouflaged station wagon. Wilson put his box of supplies into it; then he looked at Head. "Where are you going?"

"I'm going with you."

"No," Wilson said. "Because if I don't make it, then you've got to try. But stay here until you find out."

Wilson drove off. For perhaps thirty seconds Head stood looking after him. Suddenly there was the thin shriek of a falling bomb straight overhead. With one long plunging dive George Head went back inside the tunnel.

The bomb struck not twenty yards from where he had been standing.

The Japanese planes passed over. The shelling quit for awhile. And Jim Wilson returned to the Navy tunnel. He was grimy now, blood-stained, his face grim. But what he talked about was not what had happened to him. It was about the two corpsmen who had been on duty in the first-aid station when it was hit.

"Ed Hastings and Jack Kerbow," he said. "They weren't hurt, not badly. But a lot of other men were. And these two were trying to do what they could, with no supplies. Their supplies had been blown up. They were crying, both of 'em, out of anger, frustration, trying to make bandages out of their uniforms. No morphine to help the pain." And then his face twisted in a kind of grin. "I thought they were going to kiss me when I came with those supplies."

It was George Head who told this story later. He was one of sixteen men to escape from Corregidor in a small boat just before the island was captured. For a month they sailed through enemy-controlled waters, traveling by night, hiding by day among the islands. As the only hospital corpsman aboard, it was Head's job to keep the others healthy. He was in charge of getting food when they went ashore, and purifying the drinking water. Incredibly, every one of his men gained weight on the long voyage.

But the others, Jim Wilson, Ed Hastings, and Jack Kerbow, were not so lucky. With the fall of Corregidor they became Japanese prisoners.

TRAINING FOR THE MEDICAL CORPS
CHAPTER TWO

In 1940 the U.S. Army's Medical Corps had fewer than 1500 doctors, most of them based in the United States. Slightly more than two years later the Army had more than thirty times that many doctors, and they were spread over a good part of the world. The number of Navy doctors increased in the same way.

This abrupt growth was hard on both the doctors and the military. There was, of necessity, considerable confusion. Doctors were hurriedly assigned to Army or Navy hospitals in the United States. They might remain there, or they might be sent to combat duty with no military training at all. There were Navy doctors who went aboard their ships without knowing which way to look for the flag nor whom to salute. And there were Army doctors who weren't quite sure if a colonel outranked a major or if it was the other way around.

Most doctors, however, did at least have a few lectures on military life before they went into the field. Thousands of Army doctors were trained at the Medical Field School at Carlisle Barracks, Pennsylvania. And doctors assigned to special duty usually received intensive training. A doctor with the paratroopers, for example, had to be able to jump along with the soldiers. A flight surgeon had to understand

During training, Army medics practice the speedy evacuation of "wounded" comrades. Here the medics are moving the man from a collecting station to the clearing station further behind the lines. Carlisle Barracks, Medical Field Service School, February 1943. See page 97 for a similar scenario on the battlefield.

the special problems encountered in high-altitude flying and was given special training in how to treat these problems.

Both the Army and the Navy tried to send doctors who were already specialists to jobs where they could use their special training. But sometimes this was not possible. Many doctors who had specialized in the treatment of women or children found themselves on Navy ships where there wasn't a woman or child within a thousand miles.

Although a doctor might be sent into combat with little or no military training, he was, of course, already a doctor. He'd had his medical training before going into the service. This was not true of the Navy corpsmen and the Army medics—the enlisted men who helped the doctors, and who sometimes had to serve in place of doctors.

The training of the Army's medic and the Navy's corpsman was much alike. The Army, however, expected most of their medics to work in groups, under the close supervision of doctors.

In the Navy it was impossible to put a doctor on every small ship. There simply were not enough doctors. So the Navy concentrated on training men to work individually. On many ships an enlisted corpsman was the only "doctor" available. In literally thousands of cases American lives depended on the medical knowledge of some youngster who a year or two before had been going to school or working in a drug store or driving a truck. For this reason the average Navy training tended to be longer and more thorough than the Army's.

When the future corpsman joined the Navy he was, as a rule, sent first to boot camp. This was the same basic training given every sailor no matter what his future job was to be. He was taught to drill. He learned military discipline and basic seamanship. He went on long marches to toughen his muscles.

From boot camp the young hospital apprentice was sent to Hospital Corps Training School. And it was school with a vengeance. Around the world Navy men were being wounded; they needed medical help urgently. The knowledge necessary to help them had to be crammed into the heads of the future corpsmen as rapidly as possible.

The new corpsmen got up before dawn, bathed and shaved and marched off for a half-hour of exercise. By 0615 (6:15 a.m.) they were lined up for breakfast. Then back to their quarters to make their beds and stand inspection. And then to class.

There were classes in anatomy and physiology. There were classes in math and chemistry and pharmacy and hygiene and sanitation. Youngsters with no previous medical training had to learn the structure and function of the human body. They had to learn to recognize the most common diseases and to treat some wounds.

All the subjects had to be taught in such a way that they could be understood by a boy with an eighth-grade education as well as a boy who had entered the Navy directly from college. For many of the students the medical terms were so strange that it was like learning a foreign language along with the new information.

Hospital Apprentice Bentz Plagemann wrote an article in 1942 about his experience. (After the war he became a successful author.) In the article he said, "Of all the impressions of the Hospital Corps School the most vivid is the necessity for speed—a sort of ration card for time." The school itself was so new that many of the buildings were not yet finished, but they were being used anyway. And the corpsmen, Plagemann wrote, were like the buildings: used but not ready. They knew that men's lives would depend on them. They kept asking themselves, "When I go into combat, will I measure up? Will I be able to do my job?"

As a rule the new corpsmen stayed at the Hospital Corps Training School for about three months. From here they were sent to duty in various hospitals. Now they were actually working, but the training continued also. A man would work for awhile in one ward, then another, learning as he moved from job to job.

Pharmacist's Mate Sam Schiek was never taught how to give a hypodermic injection. "I was just told to go and do it," he said later. "And I did it."

But for some of the corpsmen, the simple matter of giving an injection was one of the most difficult things to learn.

One of these was a big, burly corpsman named Evanisky. He just could not bring himself to stick a needle into someone's arm. But Ensign Teresa Hayes, the Navy nurse whose job it was to teach him, was determined that be would learn. She took him by the arm and marched him across the ward to where a patient lay waiting.

"Now," she said, "you've seen me give a hundred. You do it."

Evanisky held the needle as if it were a bayonet. Slowly he approached the patient. And the patient began to yell. "Don't let him practice on me, Nurse! I'm no guinea pig! Don't let him do it!"

"All right," the nurse said. "But he's got to learn, even if I have to be the guinea pig."

Ensign Hayes gave the patient his injection. Then she marched Evanisky back to the laboratory. "Boil some water so it will be sterile," she said.

He did.

"Fill your hypo."

He did.

"All right. Now inject it into my arm."

Gritting his teeth, Evanisky jabbed the needle into the nurse's arm. He pushed down on the plunger—and Miss Hayes let out a shriek. Telling about it later she said, "I was so determined that Evanisky learn, I forgot one thing. I forgot to let the water cool. It was almost boiling when he shot it in my arm."

After some months of hospital training the corpsman might be sent to another hospital or another school for special training. He might become an x-ray or laboratory or surgical technician. Or he might be sent directly to a ship. Or he might be assigned to the Marines.

For those who went to the Marines it was like starting boot camp all over again, only worse. Now it was the same boot training that any newcomer to the Marines would experience. They drilled until many of them felt as if they were walking on their knees. Later they would go into combat like any other corpsman, unarmed except for their first-aid kit. But here, like any Marine, they had to learn to use rifles and hand grenades and mortars. They learned to crawl through mud and under barbed wire while machine guns fired a few inches above their heads. They learned to climb cargo nets on and off of ships in rolling seas.

Navy doctors who served with the Marines received much the same basic training as the enlisted corpsmen. For many a middle-aged doctor, unaccustomed to exercise, it was rough training indeed. But later it would save lives—lives of doctors and corpsmen and patients.

During this period there was little time for the Marines' corpsman to study his specialty. Later many of them might be sent to regular classes—but not all of them. One Marine doctor wrote that in the year and a half he and his corpsmen worked together there was never a formal lecture. Instead, he wrote, "We lived our work. We talked together wherever we had a chance to rest: beneath a Carolina pine, on a coral beach, in the back of a truck, in the stifling hold of a transport, in the darkness of the jungle…. Wherever we had time to lay aside our packs, a handful of us would talk medicine."

This particular group of corpsmen were assigned to the 1st Marine Division. Very soon they would have ample opportunity to test their newly learned knowledge in the dark jungles of Guadalcanal.

Training to become paratrooper field surgeons with the elite First Special Service Force, these Army doctors are thoroughly oriented to the feel of a parachute by wearing the practice harness before their first actual jump from a transport plane. Ft. William Henry Harrison training center, 1943.

GUADALCANAL
CHAPTER THREE

After the fall of the Philippines, Japanese armies swept southward. They captured Indochina, the Dutch East Indies, part of the huge island of Borneo. It seemed as if nothing could stop them. They appeared ready to capture Australia and to move eastward against Midway and Hawaii.

Then came the fight for Guadalcanal.

Guadalcanal was one of the strangest battles in American history. It was what the military calls a "meeting engagement"—a fight that takes place more by accident than by design. Before it began only a few persons had ever heard the name Guadalcanal. One of the Solomon Islands in the South Pacific, it is neither particularly large nor important. The land is shaped somewhat like a piece of paper you have crumpled in your fist and dropped. The jagged hills are covered in places by tall, thick grass, in other places by jungle. Heavy rains turn the valleys to swamps, and mosquitoes breed by the millions.

An American doctor, briefing his men on Guadalcanal just before the invasion, told them about the terrible climate, the mosquitoes, the tropical diseases, and the poisonous snakes in the jungle. When he finished he asked, "Are there any questions?"

"Yes, sir," one Marine said. "Why don't we just let the Japs keep the place?"

It was a good question. The answer was that the Japanese had started to build an airfield there. They didn't expect it to be a very important field. They wanted it merely to cover their left flank as they pushed toward Borneo and Australia.

The Americans didn't want the Japanese to have the airfield. And they did want Guadalcanal themselves as a first step toward reconquering the Philippines.

For these reasons, on August 7, 1942, the 1st Marine Division began to land on Guadalcanal. The outnumbered Japanese who were building the airfield retreated to the hills. Everything looked easy.

But then the Japanese sent in more troops. And the Americans sent more. And the Japanese sent more. And little by little Guadalcanal turned into one of the most vicious battles of the war.

It was here that American doctors and corpsmen first began to learn something about the nature of their enemy. In 1929 many nations had signed an agreement—the Geneva Convention—that medical troops would be unarmed noncombatants. They would wear large Red Crosses on their arms and helmets. Because their job was not to kill but to save lives, each side would respect the other's doctors and medics.

The Japanese, however, had not signed this agreement.

In the outfit of a captured Japanese sniper, U.S. Marine Sgt. Charles Arnton climbs a palm tree to show how a sniper hid in the treetop. Guadalcanal, c. 1942.

In the jungles of Guadalcanal a Japanese sniper might wound a Marine. When the wounded man called for help, a corpsman would go to him—and the Japanese sniper would deliberately shoot the corpsman. If a doctor or corpsman went into the jungle along with a number of Marines, the Japanese would try to shoot the medical man first. They believed it would destroy the morale of the Marines to have their medics killed. As a result, doctors and corpsmen on Guadalcanal soon ripped the Red Crosses from their sleeves and painted out the Red Crosses on their helmets. But they remained favorite targets for Japanese snipers.

The beach at Guadalcanal was already secure when the 1st Battalion of the 7th Marines came ashore. But the men knew that Japanese planes might strike at any time. The ships had to be unloaded in a hurry, and the corpsmen worked along with everyone else bringing supplies ashore, moving them inland to a coconut grove, setting up first-aid stations, and digging foxholes. Two corpsmen were assigned to each company of the battalion, one to the mortar platoon, one to the communications outfit. The other ten corpsmen and the doctors formed the battalion aid station.

In the late afternoon the ships that had brought the Marines pulled out. The tropical darkness came quickly. The new men waited for their first taste of combat.

The Japanese Navy was better trained at night fighting than the Americans. So their ships controlled the waters around the island at night, and their planes controlled the air. Before dawn, however, their ships would head northward toward other Japanese-held islands. And American ships would come up from the south to control the waters by day.

About midnight the first Japanese planes arrived. They flew high, above the reach of antiaircraft fire. The wind in the coconut palms, the sound of the surf on the beach, drowned out the far drone of their motors. Then they dropped flares, which hung high in the sky, giving off a ghostly green glare. They drifted slowly downward. In the green light the coconut palms looked huge and misshapen, their black shadows striping the ground.

Offshore, where the darkness was untouched by the flares, there was a sudden flash of light, another, and another, like sheet lightning low above the water. Seconds later came the thin scream of shells—lost instants later in the roar of one explosion after another. Japanese ships were bombarding the island. Shells ripped the coconut palms. The earth heaved with the explosions. High overhead the circling planes began to drop their bombs to add to the destruction.

On the ground the Marines tried to dig deeper into their foxholes. But even then some of them kept their sense of humor. A shell struck so close to the foxhole where Corpsman Paul Gelnett crouched with a friend that he was blown into the air and came down on his back. Stunned, he lay motionless for a while, then began to feel over his body to see if he was wounded.

"Are you hurt?" his friend called.

"No," Gelnett said. "But I'll never forget this, even if I live another two hours."

Not all the corpsmen were this lucky. A.C. Jennings, lying face down in a foxhole, heard only the shriek of the shell before he was knocked unconscious. When he came to, he was on his back. Above him a flare was drifting through the shattered palm trees. By its light he could see that his left arm was badly torn just above the wrist.

From a nearby foxhole a friend was calling to him. "Do you need help?"

But shells were still falling. Jennings did not want his friend to cross the open ground to reach him. "I'm all right," he called.

His first-aid kit lay nearby. He put a tourniquet on his arm to stop the bleeding. He applied a battle dressing to his own wound. The first person I ever treat in combat, he thought, and it has to be me.

The corpsmen had been taught that it was not their duty to go to a wounded man if, more than likely, they would be wounded themselves in the effort. "It doesn't help to have two wounded or dead men out there instead of one," the officers had told them. But it is not easy to hear a man call for help and not go to him. When Pharmacist's Mate Jim Narron heard calls for help, he waited only until there was a moment's lull in the shelling. Then he was racing between the palms, diving into a shell-hole when he heard the whine of a bomb, up and running again seconds later.

The man he found was badly wounded. As Narron put on a battle dressing and gave a shot of morphine, another corpsman joined him. Together they began to carry the wounded man toward the battalion aid station, running a few steps, dropping to the ground, moving again.

The aid station was a small, blacked-out shelter. In the stifling heat Lieutenant Commander Edward Smith and Lieutenant Schuster, Navy doctors assigned to the Marines, were already working. They knew the shelter offered no protection from a really close shell or bomb hit. They just tried to shut the thought out of their minds and concentrate on the work to be done.

After an hour or so the Japanese ships turned away. The planes left. The last flare drifted down and burned out. Now most of the Marines could hope for a few hours' rest before daylight. But the corpsmen kept searching the shattered coconut grove for more wounded. And in the breathless heat of the battalion aid station, the doctors performed one operation after another. The quicker the wounded were treated, the better their chance of survival, and the doctors kept working.

A few days later the battalion took part in a general advance against the Japanese. The men moved through the jungle in a long, narrow column. So that medical help would be near all the men, Dr. Smith marched at the front of the column. Dr. Schuster near the rear, and the corpsmen were scattered throughout.

The corpsmen were loaded down with medical supplies,

food, stretchers, and plasma; but they carried no guns. A gun cannot protect a man against enemy shells, but his power to fight back does give him confidence. It takes a special kind of courage to move unarmed against an enemy who wants to kill you. It was the kind of courage that every doctor and corpsman had to have, along with a strong belief in what they were there to do: not to kill, but to save lives.

At first the heat, the swampy jungle, and the mosquitoes were the only enemies they found. Then they came on an abandoned Japanese camp. Apparently the Japanese had left in a hurry, under attack by American planes. There were helmets, gas masks, opened and half-empty cans of food. There were also dead Japanese. One sat with his back propped against a tree, the can from which he had been eating still in his hand.

The Marines moved on. In the late afternoon they were in a valley with steep hills rising on both sides. Without warning a storm of machine-gun, rifle, and mortar fire swept the Marines. A Marine walking beside Dr. Smith suddenly pitched forward, a bullet through his foot. As Smith bent quickly over him the Marine rolled onto his back and fired past the doctor's face straight up into the palm tree overhead. When Smith looked up he saw a Japanese sniper hanging from the rope with which he had secured himself in the tree.

Orders were shouted for the Marines to fight their way to the top of a nearby hill. It was hard going through the trees and thick grass. Fire from unseen guns raked them.

For the corpsmen it was doubly hard because not one of them went alone. Crawling, each corpsman dragged or carried a wounded man with him.

The wounded outnumbered the corpsmen. When the corpsmen reached the crest of the hill, they left the wounded in care of the doctors and went back for more.

Luckily, the darkness came quickly. On the hilltop the Marines dug themselves in. The Japanese might stage a night attack; they might not. But at least there was a short time to rest. Not for the corpsmen, however. There were still more wounded men to search for in the darkness and carry back to their own lines. Here nervous sentries might shoot at anything that moved in the night, their own corpsmen as well as the enemy.

The work went on. One corpsman, carrying a wounded Marine on his back, had almost reached the top of the hill when he fainted from exhaustion. He and the wounded man rolled back down the hill. Other corpsmen went and brought them in.

About midnight it started to rain. It was cold now. The doctors and corpsmen moved among the wounded, covering them with their own coats, giving plasma and morphine. There was no chance to rest.

Next day a relief column reached the Marines on the hilltop. Dr. Schuster, along with stretcher-bearers and a few Marines for protection, began the march back to the airfield, carrying the wounded. The rest of the battalion took up the advance once more.

Snipers hidden in the trees and on top of the low hills

tried to pick off the Marines. For a half-hour the men might move steadily forward without a shot being fired. Then suddenly there would be the light, thin crack of a Japanese rifle answered by a crash of American guns. A Japanese might fall like a shot bird from the top of a palm. But also the stretcher-bearers might have another wounded Marine to carry.

Small rivers cut through the jungle. As the Marines began to wade one stream a rifle fired from the far bank. A Marine staggered and fell face down in the water. His arms and legs moved weakly as the current carried him away.

Pharmacist's Mate Jack Ture was on the riverbank and saw the Marine fall. Ture was a thin, gangling youngster

U.S. Marines move forward on Guadalcanal.

from Mississippi. He did not look strong enough to carry the pack of medical supplies strapped on his back. Now he dropped the pack, raced down the riverbank, and dived in. From the far side of the river the Japanese sniper kept firing. The bullets made small, leaping geysers around Ture's head. He reached the wounded Marine, rolled him over on his back, and pulled him to the bank.

American guns silenced the sniper. The Marine's wound was bandaged; he was placed on a stretcher. There was no way he could be sent back to the airfield now. Holding the stretcher over their heads, bearers carried the wounded man across the river, and the advance continued.

It was halted next day on the bank of another river. The Japanese were in force on the far side. Time and again the Marines tried to cross; time and again they were driven back. Finally the Marines changed their tactics. They moved down river to join up with other units near the river's mouth. What followed was one of the bloodiest battles of the entire campaign.

The Marines were on the east bank of the river. They wanted to cross and drive the Japanese westward, away from the American-held airfield. The Japanese, on the west bank, wanted to cross and drive toward the airfield to recapture it.

For days the fighting surged back and forth. Men fell in the river and on the beach and in the pounding surf just beyond the river's mouth. By day and by night the corpsmen went out—under the fire of rifles, machine guns, mortars, artillery—and brought in the wounded. An aid station was set up near the beach. The American artillery fired directly over it. The whine of the shells mingled with the clash of palm fronds in the wind, the boom of the surf, and the beating of the fierce rains that alternated with periods of glaring sunshine.

Kenneth Durant, a 23-year-old Pharmacist's Mate from Algona, Iowa, worked his way to the front lines time and again. Sometimes they were on one side of the river, sometimes the other. Durant gave first-aid to the wounded, then carried them back to the aid station. He lost track of time, of days and nights without sleep or rest. He was starting toward the river again, staggering from exhaustion, when an officer at the command post called him and told him to rest.

Durant stopped. Another minute and he would have been asleep in the sandbagged command post. But a shell hit not fifty feet away. Moments later there came the cry Durant had heard so many times: "Corpsman! Corpsman!" A man was wounded and needed help.

Durant got to his feet. The man lay near where the shell had hit, some fifteen yards from the command post. Kenneth Durant ran to him. Then a second shell hit, and both men were killed.

A Marine dive bomber, hit by Japanese fire, crashed just offshore. Twenty-year-old Corpsman Don Van Schoonhoven, of Glendale, California, jumped into the crash boat that went racing toward the plane. It was in deep water, only the tail still above the surface. Van Schoonhoven went over the side of the boat and swam to the plane. He knew the plane might sink at any moment and the suction would carry him down with it. But he dived, feeling his way along the fuselage until he reached the tail gunner's seat. The seat hood was jammed, and Van Schoonhoven could not open it. He kept trying. His lungs felt as though they were bursting. At last he got the hood open, got the gunner out and pulled him still breathing toward the crash boat.

There was no chance to go back for the pilot. The plane slipped under the waves and vanished.

On the third night of the fight at the river's mouth Dr. Edward Smith, working in the aid station, heard a scream such as he had never heard before. On the far side of the river he saw something vague and white that seemed to half race, half fly toward the water. There was a great splashing and another scream. It occurred to Dr. Smith that he had been working too long without sleep; now he must be asleep and dreaming while still standing erect. Perhaps the Marines in the foxholes along the river thought the same thing, for not a shot was fired as the ghostly object burst out of the river and straight through the American lines.

It passed within a few yards of Dr. Smith. It was a white horse. Where it came from and where it went Smith never knew.

Next day the American command decided to try an end run around the river's mouth: a detachment of Marines in small boats would circle the river's mouth, land behind the Japanese lines, and attack from the rear. Everyone knew it was a desperate chance and men were asked to volunteer.

One of the volunteers was Eugene Baxter of Fairfield, California. Baxter was a regular Navy man, a Pharmacist's Mate 1st Class who for a long time had wanted to be promoted to Chief Pharmacist's Mate. Before coming to Guadalcanal he had taken his exams, but whether he had passed them or not he did not know.

The Marines landed behind the Japanese lines without opposition. But when they started inland they walked straight into an ambush. The first burst of fire cut down half the men.

The Marines fought back. They called for fire from the American ships offshore. But gradually they were pushed back toward the beach, carrying their wounded and dead with them.

Crash boats came in to pick up the survivors. The surf was so rough that one of the boats overturned. It was difficult even for an uninjured man to fight his way through the waves alone. But time after time Gene Baxter carried a wounded Marine through the surf to the boats, and went back to the fireswept beach for another.

The motor of one of the crash boats refused to start. Baxter helped in unloading this boat and carrying the wounded men to another.

The small boats finally moved out to sea, but there was not room for all the men. Baxter volunteered to stay ashore. With several others he slipped into the jungle and eventually made his way through the enemy lines back to the east side of the river.

But the battle was still going on. Once more Baxter went to the front lines. He brought back a wounded man to the battalion aid station. Moments later he was killed by a shell.

A few days after this the word came through: he had been promoted to Chief.

While the land fighting on Guadalcanal swayed back and forth, Japanese ships continued their almost nightly bombardment of the airfield, which the Americans had renamed Henderson Field. Usually there would be one or two Japanese cruisers and several destroyers. But on the night of October 13–14 the Japanese sent down two battleships, a cruiser, and eight or nine destroyers. Later the Marines would speak of this night as "The Bombardment," as if there had never been another.

It began about an hour after midnight. A plane droned in from the sea, dropping flares. Then, far offshore, the battleships opened fire with their huge 14-inch guns. Nearer to shore the cruiser and destroyers joined in. The great shells began to fall on Henderson Field like rain. Planes were hit and burst into flame. Ammunition dumps exploded. Fires lit the area with a terrible red glare—and into this target the ships continued to pour their shells.

Hospital Corpsmen John Hunter Lee and Vernon Floyd crouched in a foxhole near the battalion aid station. The bombardment had continued for nearly an hour when another man tumbled into the foxhole. It was a corpsman named Michaels, his right hand almost torn off by shrapnel. As Floyd and Lee worked over him, Michaels told what had happened. He had been in a shelter perhaps a hundred yards away when it took a direct hit. Some of the men with him had been killed, some wounded. They needed help.

The bombardment was at its peak, the shriek of approaching shells lost in the long, rumbling roar of explosions. But Floyd and Lee left their foxhole, running, diving into holes, running again. They reached the shelter that had been hit.

The shelter had been a small trench dug in the ground, then covered by coconut logs and a large piece of boiler plate. Now it was a contorted mass of torn earth, logs, and bodies.

Later Vernon Floyd would tell about it. "We found that three of the men were dead," he said. "The others were still living, but wounded. We dug the living out of the debris and gave first aid. Of the six men we recovered, only one died. He was Dr. Ringus, who was in a state of shock from loss of blood, and we couldn't bring him around. One of the problems was getting into such a small space to remove the injured. By this time other help arrived and we carried the wounded on stretchers about one hundred yards to the first-aid station, where we continued to care for them."

Though Floyd did not mention it, shells were falling around them all this time. Every man who carried a stretcher was willingly risking his own life to save another.

Vernon Floyd and John Lee were not the only hospital corpsmen who proved to be heroes that night. Alfred Todak and Andrew Chitwood dug men from the debris of wrecked shelters at the risk of their own lives. Time after time Gerald Arrington circled the bivouac area looking for wounded men, and carried one man after another to the battalion aid station.

Flight Nurse Lt. Mae Olson takes the name of a wounded American soldier as medics place him aboard a hospital plane for prompt evacuation from Guadalcanal.

And the aid station itself offered only a little shelter. Later a Navy lieutenant told of a wild ride in a truck to get away from the shelling. As the truck raced away from the bivouac area it passed the aid station. There the lieutenant could see the doctors, still operating in the midst of shellfire.

Hospital Corpsman Vernon Floyd won a Silver Star Medal for his courage and skill on the night of "The Bombardment." One week later he was to start another adventure for which he would win the Navy and Marine Corps Medal.

For the first time in American military history, wounded men were being flown direct from the battlefield to hospitals far behind the lines. Transport planes would land on Henderson Field, casualties would be rushed on board, and the planes would take off for islands to the south. Sometimes a doctor and corpsman went with the wounded. But because of the shortage of doctors, usually only a corpsman was aboard. A little later, nurses sometimes flew with the corpsmen.

On October 20, Vernon Floyd was scheduled to make such a trip from Guadalcanal to Espiritu Santo. The hospital plane, an Army Air Force C-47, touched down on Henderson Field in the late afternoon. Immediately corpsmen began to carry patients from the sick bay bomb shelter. The plane was about half-loaded when suddenly there was the thin shriek of an incoming shell. It landed on the runway a hundred yards from the plane. Moments later a second shell landed. "Millimeter Mike," as the

Marines called the Japanese artillery hidden in the hills, was firing at the plane.

Swiftly the patients were unloaded and taken back to the bomb shelter. Millimeter Mike quit firing. The patients were brought out again. And once more Millimeter Mike opened fire. Once more the patients were hastily unloaded.

This happened three times. It was night now. Finally the patients were loaded, the runway partially repaired, and the C-47 took the air. Later Vernon Floyd would say, "The gremlins were really working this night. We had covered about one third of the distance to Espiritu Santo when we ran into a tropical storm. Our radio went out. The storm blew us off course. When finally the weather cleared and the navigator could get a fix on our location, it was almost daybreak. We were about a hundred miles northwest of New Caledonia, and down to our last few gallons of gas."

Below them was a long coral reef. From the air it showed only as a white line of breaking water against the blue sea. The pilot took the plane down lower, looking for a place where the coral came above the surface. There wasn't one.

"Do what you can for the patients," the pilot told Floyd. "Our gas is gone. We'll have to ditch in a couple of minutes."

"Yes, sir."

There were sixteen patients on the plane. Some were wounded. Others had severe cases of malaria. And several were victims of battle fatigue—men who had broken mentally under the long days and nights of fighting on Guadalcanal. In the plane they had believed themselves on the way to safety—but now this. How would they react when they learned the plane was going down at sea?

Floyd spoke to them calmly. He made sure that all the patients had their safety belts fastened. Then he began to secure every loose object that might go flying through the air on impact. There wasn't much time. The plane had circled and turned into the wind. The ocean seemed to be rushing up to meet them.

Later Floyd said, "Things were happening so fast I can't recall having any particular thoughts, except to try to prevent further injuries." At the last moment he flung himself on the deck, his back braced against a bulkhead.

The plane hit the water, bounced like a skipped rock, hit again, and her nose went down. The impact flattened Floyd against the bulkhead. Something, he did not know what, tore loose from overhead and crashed against him.

Later, Floyd would learn he had three broken ribs. But now there was no time to think about it. He was on hands and knees crawling along the fuselage, trying to find out what had happened.

The plane had gone into the sea directly over the coral reef, at a point where the water was about five feet deep. The tail, part of one wing, and most of the fuselage were above the surface. For the moment anyway the plane seemed safe enough.

Quickly Floyd checked his patients. Only two had been hurt in the landing. One had a dislocated shoulder, the other a bad cut on the back. There wasn't much Floyd could do about the shoulder, but he put a battle dressing on the cut. He assured the battle-fatigue cases that everything was going to be all right. He put new bandages on the wounded who needed them. Then he crawled out on the wing to consult with the plane's crew.

The radio operator had got off an SOS before the plane went into the sea, but whether it had been heard no one knew. There was no way of knowing how long before they would be found, if at all.

"We'll try to rig up an emergency radio," the pilot said, "and send distress signals." He looked at Floyd. "How much food and water do we have?"

There was very little food, and only about two gallons of water for sixteen patients plus the crew. "I'll try to make some sort of still," Floyd said, "to distill seawater."

He set to work. His broken ribs were hurting now, but he tried to forget them. He found a gallon can, some aluminum tubing.

As he worked a new danger presented itself. The plane had crashed at low tide. But now the tide was rising and little by little it covered the plane until only the tail was above the surface, with everybody crowded into or hanging onto it. If a storm came at high tide the plane might break apart and wash away.

By the next day Vernon Floyd had finished his still. He used de-icer fluid for fuel. How long this would last he did not know, but meanwhile he could distill a few pints of fresh water each day.

The days passed slowly. Once the pilot shot a large fish swimming close to the plane, and the men ate raw fish. When a rainstorm swept over them, Floyd climbed onto the wing and held an oilcloth over his head. The cloth funneled the rain into a bucket held by one of the crew. That relieved the water shortage, at least for a time. One of the malaria patients was growing worse, but fortunately they had quinine, so Floyd was able to check the attack. The men suffering from battle fatigue needed almost constant reassurance. Bandages had to be changed on the wounded.

No one had thought much of the days of the week until one of the wounded men said, "You know, it's Sunday." Many of the men in the wrecked plane had not been to church for months, or even years. But suddenly Sunday was important to all of them. The navigator had a Bible. Someone asked him to read aloud from it.

All the men were crowded into the tail of the wrecked plane; the sea surrounded them, white where the waves broke over the reef, blue beyond to the horizon. There was no sound except that of the waves and the voice of the navigator as he read:

And seeing the multitudes, he went up into a mountain: and when he was set, his disciples came unto him: And he opened his mouth, and taught them, saying,

Blessed are the poor in spirit: for theirs is the kingdom of heaven.

Blessed are they that mourn: for they shall be comforted.

Blessed are the meek: for they shall inherit the earth.

After this the men held a brief religious service every day. It did not matter that they were of different faiths. Such differences were unimportant on the face of the lonely sea.

On the tenth day an Army Air Force plane found them. As it circled, all the men in the wrecked plane tried to crowd onto the wings and wave.

The Army plane circled and came low to drop supplies. These fell into the water and began to drift away. Floyd, along with some of the crew, dived in to get them.

The surf was running strongly. Pain from his broken ribs stabbed Floyd as he swam. But he got one bundle of the supplies and started back toward the plane. A wave hurled him against the coral reef and the jagged edges ripped his legs. He managed to get back to the plane, but by the next day the cuts on his legs were becoming infected.

That afternoon three Navy PBY flying boats came over. The weather was rough now, the waves high as they broke over the reef. Even so, the PBYs put down on the surface some distance away. They taxied in close to the reef, then launched rubber rafts in which men paddled to the wrecked plane.

Now there was the job of loading the sick and wounded men into the rafts and getting them back to the PBYs. Charged with the care of the wounded, Vernon Floyd was the last man off the reef.

And still it was not over. A wave swept one of the PBYs against a reef, cutting the hull. It began to fill with water. Now everyone aboard had to be moved from this plane to the other two. Overloaded, in rough seas, the two remaining PBYs could not take off.

A Catalina PBY-5 takes off in 1943.

Next day a destroyer came over the horizon. Once more Vernon Floyd had to oversee the transfer of his wounded men. But at long last it was over. On board the destroyer he could get treatment for his own cuts and broken ribs. By now the infection in his legs was so bad that he would bear the scars all his life. But the sixteen sick and wounded men who had been under his care all came through the ordeal, only slightly the worse for wear.

The fighting on Guadalcanal would continue for another three months. But by February 1943 the Japanese high command had decided that the island was not worth the cost. Under cover of darkness they withdrew what troops they could, and left Guadalcanal in American hands.

THE LOSS OF A PORTABLE HOSPITAL
CHAPTER FOUR

In September 1942, while the fighting on Guadalcanal was still going strong, Japanese forces were landing on the jungle-clad coast of New Guinea, some 600 miles to the west. The Japanese plan was to capture the eastern end of this big island, and from there to move south to attack Australia. To prevent this, both the United States and Australia had sent troops to fight the Japanese in New Guinea. Base hospitals were set up in Australia, and wounded men were brought here from the jungle fighting.

There was, however, a desperate need for hospitals closer to the actual war. So when Major Parker Hardin of Rockford, Illinois, received orders to choose a few men from one of the large hospitals in Australia and form a new, experimental unit, he could be fairly sure what it meant. His new unit, called the 22nd Portable Hospital, would soon be moving into combat.

Dr. Hardin chose his three officers with care. He would be the commanding officer and surgeon. Captain George Pugsley was anesthetist. Lieutenant Albert Rogers was chief of medicine. The assistant surgeon was Lieutenant

Leonard Milcarek. He was the youngest officer in the group, only a few years out of medical school.

Dr. Hardin chose his twenty-five enlisted medics with equal care. And as soon as the unit was formed, he began several weeks of intensive training. Veterans from the New Guinea fighting were brought in to give lectures on jungle living. There were repeated drills in how to pack and carry the hospital equipment; how to unpack fast and set up the hospital in daylight or darkness; how to pitch tents in the dark of a howling rainstorm, and take them down again.

There was also hard physical training. Later the official history of the 22nd Portable would say:

> Besides gradually increasing daily calisthenics, drill, and long full-pack marches, the entire unit did increasingly strenuous cross-country running each morning, tumbling, unarmed combat, etc. On several occasions all personnel, led by Major Hardin [the Major was forty-three years old, the oldest man in the outfit] ran through the 600-yard Australian assault obstacle course at Camp Redbank. This consisted of 12-foot vertical jump, 10-foot broad jump from eight-foot height, ditches, obstacles, fences, etc., and ended with climbing a 20-foot pole and going across a 75-foot rope.

There were also many swimming and life-saving drills. Most of the men became good swimmers. But Captain George Pugsley simply could not learn to swim. He tried; he worked at it. But the best he could do was to stay afloat for a short time.

In October new orders came through. The 22nd Portable was flown across the Coral Sea to Pongami, in New

ABOVE: In the New Guinea jungle, wounded American soldiers wait on crude litters to be transferred to base hospitals in Australia. BELOW: Administering blood plasma to a wounded soldier at the portable hospital in New Guinea, 1942.

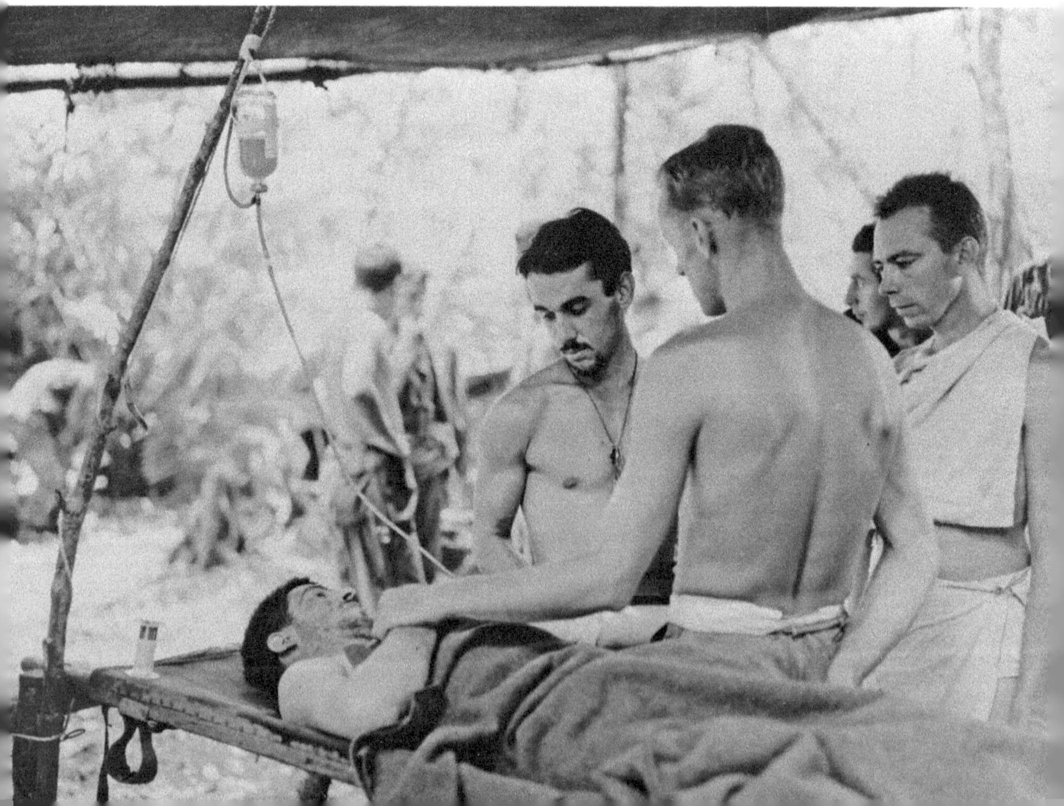

Guinea. From here a small coastal vessel carried them to Oro Bay, close behind the fighting. Then, on November 16, the 22nd went aboard another small ship, the *Alacrity*. Her decks were jammed with the hospital's equipment, with gasoline, ammunition, the men of the 22nd, and with forty or more New Guinea natives. Behind the *Alacrity* came three other small ships, all filled with soldiers.

The *Alacrity*'s skipper was an Australian, not too well acquainted with the coast of New Guinea. In the late afternoon his ship lay about a half-mile off the coast, and the skipper had a problem. All he could see was a narrow shoreline with jungle rising beyond it. He didn't know whether he had gone past the American lines into Japanese-held territory or not. So he circled slowly, watching the coast and trying to make up his mind. Behind him followed the other three small ships.

Down the coast from the northwest came a flight of airplanes. They were high, about 15,000 feet. The Americans watched them nervously.

"I was with a fighter squadron for awhile," Dr. Milcarek said. "I know every kind of fighter we have in this area. Those aren't American fighters."

"Then let's hope they are American bombers," Dr. Hardin said.

The planes passed over, still high. The men on the boats sighed with relief—then caught their breaths. A mile or so to the southeast the planes had turned. The large formation began to break up into three-plane units, getting lower. One of the units straightened out and headed for the ships. And still nobody knew whose the planes were.

Then came the answer. Along the leading edge of the plane wings lights began to flicker as the planes' guns were fired. Machine-gun bullets lashed at the water around the four small ships. Bullets slashed into the deck and cabin of the *Alacrity*, starting fires. Then the first flight of planes had passed, the Rising Sun of Japan clear on their fuselages. Close behind the first flight came a second.

It was the 22nd's first taste of combat. And for a few moments the men ran in crazy circles searching for some place to hide, to get away from the bullets. But on the small, crowded ship there was no safe place. The New Guinea natives were screaming, some of them already jumping over the side of the ship.

A single machine gun was mounted on the *Alacrity*. As the second flight of planes came over, William Vana, a medic who had never fired a machine gun before, ran to it. Somehow he got it firing. But without training, he did not aim far enough in front of the planes. The red stream of his tracers followed the planes but did not hit them.

Fires on the *Alacrity* were spreading. The ammunition and gasoline on the deck began to explode. Within moments the little ship was a mass of flame. So were the three following ships.

Major Hardin gave the order to abandon ship. Rapidly men began to dive over the side and swim toward shore.

Captain Pugsley could not swim. But he knew he could not stay on the ship and live. He jerked off his clothes, climbed over the rail, looked down at the water for one long moment, and jumped.

When he came to the surface Dr. Rogers was beside him. "Take it easy," Rogers said. "Turn on your back and float. You can do that. And I'll tow you ashore." They made it safely to shore.

Dr. Milcarek had gone into the water with all his clothes on. He was a good swimmer, but the shore was a long way off. Rapidly he stripped off his clothes, let go his heavy shoes. All around him men were doing the same.

Another flight of planes came over, strafing the men in the water. Milcarek saw one man hit in the head, throw up his arms, and sink. There was no chance to reach him.

Dive bombers followed the fighter planes. Dr. Milcarek did not see the first bomber. He was swimming when suddenly he felt as though the water around him had turned into an iron band crushing his chest. He lost consciousness.

How long he was unconscious he did not know. It could have been only a few moments. Then he was moving again, trying to draw air into his aching lungs. He realized that it was the impact of a bomb that had knocked him unconscious, and he knew that an underwater explosion could cause serious internal injury to a nearby swimmer. So now he tried to watch for the dive bombers. When he saw a bomb falling he rolled swiftly on his back, lifting as much of his body out of the water as possible. This made him a better target for the strafing, but the bomb's explosion only tossed him out of the water without injury.

Dr. Hardin had also gone into the water wearing his clothes. He was an excellent swimmer. At Princeton he had played on the water-polo team, and he had been a professional lifeguard during the summers. But like Dr. Milcarek he did not know that some of the Japanese planes were carrying bombs. So instead of immediately swimming toward shore, he swam close alongside the *Alacrity*. He hoped the hull of the ship would protect him from strafing until the planes had gone. Then the first bomb exploded nearby.

Hardin could not tell how close it was. He did not even know it was a bomb. He only knew that something struck him a tremendous blow. For a time, he was unable to breathe or think. Later he would say, "I vaguely remember coming up and going down several times. I could only feel a kind of amazement and terror. It began to occur to me that I was going to drown rather than be killed by the strafing."

Gradually his head cleared. He began to swim for shore, watching for the bombs as Lieutenant Milcarek had done.

The water grew shallow some distance from the beach. As Dr. Hardin waded toward the beach he saw a man floating in the surf. Hardin caught him and pulled him ashore. Other men lay on the beach, some in the water. Some were men of the 22nd, some were from the other ships sunk with the *Alacrity*. All those who could walk helped pull the others from the water. They carried them into the edge of the jungle where they would be hidden from the Japanese planes.

Just behind lines in New Guinea, in a crude jungle operating room and with a minimum of equipment, the doctor Major George Marks and a medic operate on a soldier whose arms were wounded by shrapnel.

There were no medical supplies. All had been lost with the *Alacrity*. Most of the men were naked. The medics who had any clothing at all ripped it into strips to make bandages for the wounded. Sergeant Hart, the unit's chief medical technician, had been badly wounded in the back, but now he kept working with the others to help the more seriously injured.

Not far from the beach there was an abandoned native village, the small huts built on stilts high above the ground. The wounded men were carried here and put on the ground beneath the huts. By now it was dark and raining. The men felt their way through the darkness to find banana fronds with which to cover the wounded.

Quite suddenly out of the darkness came a man in uniform, carrying a light. It was Lieutenant Paul Maurer, an Army dentist. From a distance he had seen the attack on the ships, and had hurried through the jungle with all the morphine and bandages he could carry. Stretcher-bearers arrived later.

Of the twenty-nine officers and men in the 22nd Portable Hospital, four had been killed, five badly wounded. All the supplies and records had been lost. Few of the men had any clothing, except what was given to them by other soldiers. But they were still trained doctors and medics. The wounded were sent back to an evacuation hospital. The twenty uninjured doctors and corpsmen went forward to join another of the new portable hospitals—and to carry on their work.

SOLOMONS, GILBERTS, AND OTHER PACIFIC ISLANDS
CHAPTER FIVE

With the capture of Guadalcanal and the American advance along the coast of New Guinea, the tide of battle in the Pacific began to turn, very slowly, against the Japanese. Inch by inch, island by island, the Americans fought their way northward through the Solomons. It was vicious, bloody fighting every step of the way. But wherever there was fighting, there were also the noncombatants, the doctors and enlisted men whose job was to save lives, even though it might be at the cost of their own. One of those who gave his own life to save others was Private Frank J. Petrarca, of Cleveland, Ohio.

In July 1943, Petrarca was serving with the medical detachment of the 145th Infantry, 37th Infantry Division, on New Georgia Island. When his unit moved up a jungle-clad hill against the Japanese lines, Private Petrarca went with them. They moved slowly, flat against the ground, crawling from tree to tree, from shellhole to shellhole, raked by rifle, machine-gun, and mortar fire. But within a hundred yards of the Japanese lines the unit was pinned down. Unable to advance, the men lay motionless, waiting for their own artillery to fire over them into the Japanese lines.

Between the two forces three Americans lay wounded. Petrarca saw them. He saw, too, the flash of the Japanese guns. He saw an occasional hand grenade arch out of the Japanese lines and roll toward the wounded men. Nobody could stay alive long in that exposed position.

With his first-aid pouch in his hands, Frank Petrarca crawled out of his shellhole. For perhaps ten yards he had some protection from trees. Then he was in the open, wriggling across the ground, keeping so flat he seemed almost to have buried himself. Japanese guns opened fire on him. Bullets flicked the top of his shirt; they kicked dirt in his face.

Finally Petrarca reached the first of the three wounded men. Nearby was a shallow dip in the earth and Petrarca dragged the wounded man into it. A quick examination showed that he had been shot through the side. Petrarca slashed the man's clothing, sprinkled sulfa in the wound, and put on a battle dressing.

But two wounded men were still in the open. Petrarca crawled out of the hole, across the ground to the nearest man, and dragged him back. Once more there was a quick examination, sulfa, a tourniquet and battle dressing. Then once more Private Frank Petrarca was in the open, crawling toward the wounded man who lay less than seventy-five yards from the Japanese. Bullets skimmed his back and slashed the dirt around him. Incredibly he was not touched.

The wounded man had been hit by a mortar, wounded in half a dozen places. Petrarca knew the man could not survive being dragged across the rough ground. But something had to be done. Blood came in slow spurts from a cut artery in the man's leg.

Petrarca moved so that he lay between the wounded man and the Japanese guns, shielding the man with his own body. He groped for the cut artery and tried to stop the bleeding by pressure.

To the rear, American artillery was firing. The shells whistled over Petrarca's head and smashed into the Japanese lines less than seventy-five yards from him. Covered by the barrage, the men of the 145th advanced. When the barrage lifted, they overran the Japanese lines.

The soldier whom Petrarca shielded had died. So the medic, still uninjured, went back to the two wounded men in the nearby depression. He stayed with them until litter-bearers arrived. Then Petrarca went forward again after his unit.

It was two days later that the 145th was caught in intense mortar fire. Petrarca, crouching in a foxhole, heard a shell explode less than twenty yards away, almost on top of a hole where Petrarca knew his sergeant was hiding.

"Sarge!" he called. "Sarge, are you all right?"

There was no answer. Raising his head, Petrarca saw the sergeant's foxhole was almost filled with debris, the sergeant himself more than half buried, face down. Petrarca raced toward him, dived as another shell smashed close by. Snatching off his helmet, he began to dig, uncovering the sergeant's face. He was still conscious. Petrarca piled up enough dirt to give some protection while he dressed the sergeant's wounds. Then he stayed with him until the barrage ended.

This was on July 29, 1943. Two days later the 145th was again advancing. There was a low, steep ridge. Some of the men reached the top of it, and were cut down. One fell on the far side. Petrarca, huddled with the rest of his unit near the foot of the ridge, heard the man's cry, "Medic! Medic!" Petrarca started up the ridge.

A soldier stopped him. "You can't go over that crest!" he yelled. "You can't. Nobody can."

"I've got to help him," Petrarca said.

He crawled forward. But the crest of the ridge was a wall of Japanese fire. Machine-gun bullets ripped into Petrarca. He kept going. He was hit again. And again. He quit crawling and got to his feet, wavering, stumbling, still trying to reach the wounded man. And then he fell.

Posthumously, Private Frank J. Petrarca was awarded the Congressional Medal of Honor, the highest award his country has to give.

★

Captain Isbin S. Giddens, a young doctor from Ray City, Georgia, was also on New Georgia Island. He was assigned to a first-aid station, set up a few hundred yards behind the lines in whatever shelter was available. Here he worked on the wounded brought in by the litter-bearers.

At least, that was the way it usually went. But late one afternoon a medic came stumbling into the station, breathing hard.

"Doc," he panted, "we've got a man up front that needs your help bad. He's shot through the throat. Cut the external jugular vein. It's not bleeding as much as I thought it would—but plenty bad. We don't dare move him."

Having left the comparative safety of their foxhole under heavy Japanese fire, two Marines on Tarawa return with a wounded comrade.

Giddens wasted no time on questions. He grabbed his surgical kit, some plasma bottles, and followed the medic. It was rough going through a forest of shattered coconut palms. Artillery shells passed overhead in both directions. Ahead of the two men mortars were firing. The explosions mixed with the light, thin chatter of Japanese machine guns and the hoarse sound of heavier-caliber American guns.

"Watch out for snipers. Doc," the medic said. "These trees are lousy with 'em."

"Hurry," Giddens said.

The wounded man lay in a narrow slit trench. A medic kneeling beside him held a plasma bottle with one hand, the needle in the man's arm with the other.

"Good," Giddens said.

It was growing dark. Using his flashlight Giddens examined the wound. The bullet had cut the vein cleanly and the ends had collapsed, slowing the bleeding. Lucky, Giddens thought, or the man wouldn't still be alive. Handing the flashlight to the second medic, Giddens said, "Keep the light on the wound."

It had started to rain, a sudden, tropic downpour. The slit trench gave slight protection. The raindrops shimmered in the thin beam of light that shone on the open wound, the man's shoulder, the blood stained earth beneath. The doctor and medics were almost lost in the gloom.

They had no sterile operating gowns, no elaborate tray of instruments handled by trained nurses. Saying a silent prayer that sulfa would prevent infection, Giddens went to work. He clamped off the ends of the vein. Carefully, precisely, he sutured the vein together. He removed the clamps, and saw the blood begin to flow through the repaired vein.

It was still raining. Dr. Giddens placed a battle dressing over the wound. With some of his own clothing and some from the medics he rigged a kind of shelter over the wounded man.

Still, the patient could not be moved. All night Dr. Giddens and the medics stayed beside him. They knew the

Japanese might overrun the trench at any time. However, with morning the Japs were pushed back. Litter-bearers arrived and the wounded man was taken safely back to a field hospital.

While the fighting pressed northward in the South Pacific, the Navy started a second drive toward Japan in November 1943. This one was headed almost straight west across the Central Pacific. The first place selected for invasion was Tarawa, a small, almost unknown atoll in the Gilbert Islands. The Japanese, however, had fortified it strongly. The U.S. Navy still had a lot to learn about amphibious operations—and at Tarawa almost everything that could go wrong, went wrong.

The plan was for ships and planes to bombard the little island until the Japanese fortifications were destroyed. Then the Marines would land and take over. But the Japanese fortifications were far stronger than any Americans had thought. Reinforced concrete bunkers, buried deep in the coral sand, withstood the bombardment with only minor damage. When the Marine landing boats moved toward the beach, the Japanese opened fire on them with cannon, mortars, machine guns, and rifles.

Very little had been known about the waters around Tarawa. Some of the assault boats, attempting to pass through the coral reef into the lagoon, got hung up on the coral. Some ran aground in shallow water a half-mile from shore. There the heavy guns of the Japanese smashed them to splinters.

The Marines had to leave their boats and wade. Mortar shells burst around them, throwing great geysers into the air. Machine-gun bullets made shrill whining noises as they ricocheted across the blue and silver water, dimpling it like heavy rain. Hidden snipers picked off the wading Marines one at a time.

Hospital Apprentice Hayward Skaggs, from Deer Creek, Oklahoma, was just two months past his nineteenth birthday. His assault boat was one of the first. Even so, by the time it began to worm its way through the coral reef there were already smashed boats to left and right. Wounded Marines staggered through the waist-deep water sometimes dropping into deep potholes. Dead men floated past, half submerged.

The assault boat raced toward the beach. Then, five hundred yards from shore, it struck a coral head and stuck fast. Almost immediately Japanese mortars opened fire on it.

The Marines poured over the side. The beach was still more than a quarter-mile away; but on the beach, just back from the water's edge, was a bank of sand that offered some slight protection. So at this point the beach was safer than the water.

A machine-gun bullet hit one of the Marines. He stumbled and went under.

Hayward Skaggs was heading for the beach as fast as he could, low in the water. He saw the Marine fall, and turned and went for him. Holding the man's face above water, Skaggs began to tow him toward the beach.

Another Marine was hit and went down. Skaggs

grabbed him. Now it was all he could do to keep the heads of the two men above the surface. There was almost no time to think about how much of his own body was exposed.

An assault boat that had discharged its men on the beach came by, heading back toward the open sea and the fleet. Skaggs shouted and the boat stopped. The two wounded men were pulled aboard.

"You coming with them?" the coxswain shouted to Skaggs.

Skaggs shook his head. His unit was moving toward the beach.

"All right," the helmsman shouted. "I'm getting out." And he gunned the boat toward open water.

Once more Hayward Skaggs turned toward the shore. But there were more wounded Marines in the water. He got two of them. Wading, pulling the wounded after him, he stepped into a deep pothole. His own life jacket held him up, but one of the wounded men began to go under. Floundering back into shallow water, Skaggs put his jacket on the wounded Marine. Minutes later another assault boat stopped and picked up the wounded. Skaggs did not think to recover his jacket.

How many wounded men Hayward Skaggs saved, no one knew. The crews of assault boats remembered him, pulling wounded Marines through the water, staggering from exhaustion, never getting to the comparative shelter of the beach because he was working with men who would have drowned without his help.

And then he was not there. No one saw him go under.

At Tarawa. ABOVE: Hospital corpsmen and Marines use a rubber landing raft to tow some of their wounded comrades out to a larger craft.
BELOW: Corpsmen apply traction to the fractured leg of a wounded Marine.

When the vicious battle for Tarawa was over and the Marines controlled the island, the official report on Hayward Skaggs could say only that he was "missing after action." But no Marine who saw him that day would ever forget his heroism.

After Tarawa the Navy's drive continued westward, island by slow, bloody island. On every one of them the Medical Corps furnished more than its share of heroes. In one outfit fifteen out of seventeen hospital corpsmen received medals for bravery. Casualties ran high, sometimes higher than among the fighting men. Just as they had done on Guadalcanal, the Japanese made a point of shooting the unarmed men who wore the Red Cross, the symbol of help and mercy.

There were occasional exceptions. On Saipan word came to a battalion aid station that a sniper had shot down a man on the open beach, then had shot a Marine who tried to reach him. The sniper was still there, but the wounded men needed help.

In the aid station. Lieutenant Commander Bristol Nelson looked at his corpsman, Blaine Rideout.

Rideout said, "I'll go, sir."

"You can't bring them in alone," the doctor said. "I'll go with you."

They were an unusual pair. Before the war Bristol Nelson had been one of the most famous doctors in the United States. He had been on the staff of three Boston hospitals and a professor in the Harvard Medical School. Blaine

Rideout had been equally well known as an athlete, the holder of the American record for the mile. Now they started down the beach, both knowing there was no possible way to reach the wounded men without being seen by the sniper.

And yet no shot was fired. The sniper was still there; he shot at others. But he did not shoot at the doctor and corpsman. No one could say why.

The Japanese believed it was a disgrace to be captured. Also, many of them thought that, if captured, they would be killed. More than one wounded Japanese used his last grenade to destroy himself and the hospital corpsman who was trying to save his life.

But again there were exceptions. On Guadalcanal, Dr. Edward Smith had just finished bandaging a wounded Japanese when he saw the man had a pistol in his pocket, his hand on the pistol. But the Japanese could not bring himself to kill the doctor who was helping him.

On Attu an American doctor worked for several days to save the life of a Japanese prisoner with a badly mangled leg. As the prisoner began to improve, the doctor noticed his strange actions. Each time the doctor entered the room, the prisoner would shut his eyes, turn his head away, and fold his hands. The doctor got an interpreter to ask why. It turned out that the Japanese was praying for the doctor who had saved his life.

As always in a war there were humorous incidents mixed in with the suffering and death.

On Peleliu 19-year-old Pharmacist's Mate 3rd Class William Stanburg was crouching over a wounded Marine when a large shell hit his hip pocket, ripped the seat out of his pants, struck the ground between his feet—and didn't explode.

Telling about it later he said, "I was embarrassed. But happy."

On Eniwetok a wounded Marine looked up at the two filthy, bearded corpsmen about to put him on a stretcher, and shook his head. "I've been lying here all day," he said, "waiting for some beautiful nurse to come take care of me. And I get you two guys." He added quickly, "But I'll go with you. I'll go."

Pharmacist's Mate 1st Class Sumner Quimby took part in the invasion of Guam and Okinawa, going through some of the most desperate fighting of the war. But the things he liked to tell about later were all touched with humor. His first night on Guam, he said, was spent in a foxhole close to the Japanese lines. In the early darkness he saw, or thought he saw, a Japanese sniper in a palm tree close ahead. So all night young Quimby lay motionless, watching the sniper—until in the gray light of dawn he saw it was a palm frond and not a sniper at all.

A few nights after this, Quimby and two other corpsmen were in a shellhole that had been converted to an aid station when they heard something moving toward them. They drew their knives and waited. And over the edge of the hole came, not Japanese soldiers, but several large land crabs, staring down at them with eyes that stood out on stems.

After the war Sumner Quimby went back to school. Influenced by his war experiences, he studied medicine and became a doctor.

Another young man who had his career altered by the war was Dr. Jack Ewing of Mobile, Alabama. He joined the Navy while still in medical school, did his internship in a Navy hospital, then was sent to join the fleet. On Tinian he was put to work with patients who had cracked under the strain of battle.

Dr. Ewing had no psychiatric training at this time, but he found the work fascinating. "There are many casualties in a war," he said later, "that have nothing to do with fighting or a fear of death. Sometimes worry and fear of what is happening at home can be worse than fear of battle." One of Ewing's patients was a boy in his early twenties who hadn't heard from his wife in months. He didn't know where she and his baby son were. Telling the doctor about it, he began to cry. And Dr. Ewing began to cry too.

"It took me a long time," he says, "to learn that I could give the patient more help if I did not let myself become emotionally involved."

Dr. Ewing did learn. After the war he went back to do more study and became a psychiatrist. "Medical knowledge," he says, "was advanced in many ways by the war. There were new operational techniques and new medicines. And certainly society's understanding of mental health was advanced by fifty years."

Marines in their aptly named living quarters on Tarawa.

THE BEACHHEAD AT ANZIO
CHAPTER SIX

In the early days of the war most of the fighting against the Japanese was carried on in the Pacific by the United States Navy. But on the other side of the world, the land soldiers of the American and British armies were fighting against the Germans and Italians. For the Americans, this fighting began with an invasion of North Africa where the British and Germans were already fighting one another. Here great tank battles swept back and forth across the desert, and the stretcher-bearers, the ambulances, even the hospitals had to race to keep up with the fighting.

When, finally, the Germans were driven out of Africa, the American and British armies invaded Italy. Throughout the long, cold autumn of 1943 they fought their way slowly northward. This was rugged, mountainous country and the going was bloody. So the Allied high command decided to stage an end run: troops would be taken by ship to the little town of Anzio, behind the German lines. From here they would drive inland. The German troops either would be caught between two forces and destroyed, or would have to withdraw rapidly northward.

That was the plan. It didn't quite work. As Sir Winston Churchill, the British Prime Minister, would later write, the idea was to "hurl a wildcat on the shore" to tear the vitals of the enemy. But what the allies actually got, Churchill said, was "a stranded whale."

The medical plan for the invasion was the same one followed in the Pacific. Litter-bearers and a few doctors would go in with the first troops. Individual doctors and medics would set up battalion aid stations within a few yards of the front lines—in a shellhole, a clump of trees, behind a house, wherever any shelter was available. Litter-bearers would drag or carry the wounded to the aid stations, where doctors and medics would give first aid. Then seriously wounded men would be carried—by jeep, if possible, or on stretchers—to a collecting station a little farther back. From here ambulances would carry them, if necessary, to a field hospital or an evacuation hospital. Here the men could receive treatment until they could be moved to a general hospital far behind the fighting.

At Anzio everything started well. The Germans were caught completely by surprise. Allied troops, with their advance medical detachments, went ashore against almost no opposition. In fact there was so little fighting that some of the medical units were kept on the invasion ships in order to make room on the beach for more troops and supplies.

However, General John Lucas, in command of the invasion, did not send his men racing inland. He was afraid of a German trap. He wanted to make sure his beachhead was secure. He lost precious time. And the Germans used

U.S. Coast Guardsmen load an ambulance aboard their transport as they prepare to sail for Italy.

this time to rush thousands of soldiers into the area. The American and British invaders were caught in a trap about fifteen miles long and seven miles wide at its widest point. Beyond this line hills rose sharply. German artillery in the hills could shell every inch of the beachhead, as well as the ships in the harbor beyond.

This was the situation in which the 95th and 93rd Evacuation Hospitals, along with several other units, found themselves.

The hospital area was established in a park near the beach. It would have been a lovely spot—in peacetime. The buildings were comfortable. There were plenty of shade trees, and a beautiful view of the harbor.

But the harbor was crowded with American shipping;

supplies were piled on the beach; antiaircraft guns ringed the hospital. And German planes and artillery were attacking all of them. Bombs and shells shook the buildings, cracked the walls, and split the roofs. In one 24-hour period there were twenty air raids, and shrapnel from the American guns fell over the park. Sergeant Louis Bliss of the 93rd Evacuation Hospital was hit in the head by flying shrapnel. German planes sank a hospital ship in the harbor, killing Dr. John Adams and Medic Theron McCombs.

The shelling and bombing went on, day and night. The buildings began to shatter. Wounded men brought to the hospital to be "safe" were wounded again and sometimes killed.

It was decided to move the hospital. In the limited area available there wasn't much choice of a site. Tents were set up in an open field. Now they were in clear view of the German artillery in the hills. However the tents were marked with huge Red Crosses, and the Germans did, as a rule, respect the Geneva Convention by which medical units were not to be attacked. The trouble was that, in this new location the hospital was still surrounded by legitimate military targets. There was a small airfield directly in front of it. There was a battery of American artillery directly behind it. Just off to one side was a gasoline dump.

German guns fired at the military targets, and German planes bombed them. Far too often the shells and bombs fell in the hospital area.

Now another problem arose. The hospital was set up on the edge of a swamp. The land was marshy. When the medics tried to dig foxholes, the holes filled with water.

And the canvas hospital tents offered no protection against flying shrapnel. More patients received additional wounds. Doctors and medics, and nurses who worked alongside them, were wounded and killed. It got so bad that one of the major jobs of the medics was to calm the wounded men brought to the hospital area. Many of them asked to be released and sent back to the fighting.

"At least," one of them said, "up there I can dig a foxhole and get in it. I can fight back. But here, I just have to lie still and take it."

It rained much of the time. In the nearby swamp and in the stagnant water in the shellholes, mosquitoes bred by the millions. Malaria can sometimes do more damage to an army than shells and bombs. So now the medical units had to start a war of their own—against mosquitoes. At night men slipped between the lines to spray the swamp and ditches. They filled bags with sand, dipped them in oil, and dropped the bags in slow-running drainage ditches. The oil seeped out of the bags to make a film over the water and kill mosquito larvae. One medic found an abandoned plow, hitched it to an Army tractor, and while the German guns fired at him he cleared a weed-clogged ditch so the water flowed freely and the mosquitos could not breed.

For the 95th Evacuation Hospital, February 7, 1944, turned out to be the worst day in its history. All day casualties had been brought in from the battlefield. By mid-afternoon the wards, operating and receiving tents were filled, with more ambulances still arriving. Overhead an air raid was going on, but air raids were always going on.

At 1545 (3:45 p.m.) Private Wesley Tanner was helping to carry a patient to the x-ray tent when the growing shriek of airplane engines made him look up. Down the beachhead came a German bomber with two British Spitfires right after it. The bomber turned hard right, then left again. But the British fighters stayed with it. Both opened fire, the machine guns along the wings flashing like Fourth of July sparklers. Tracers whipped past the German bomber—and straight toward the hospital area.

Desperately the bomber dived to get away from the fighters. At the same time the German pilot dumped his bombs. Almost certainly he did this in order to lighten the plane—not to attack the hospital. Probably neither the German nor the British pilots ever knew they were over the hospital. But, one after another, five bombs slid from the belly of the German plane and slanted down toward the hospital tents below.

Private Wesley Tanner saw them and shouted a warning. But there was no time to carry the patient to a foxhole. Tanner and the other litter-bearer simply placed the stretcher on the ground. Then Private Tanner lay down, covering the patient's body with his own.

The string of bombs ripped through the 95th Evacuation Hospital. One of them struck squarely on the large canvas Red Cross spread out on the ground. One landed only a few feet from the headquarters tent, another close to the pre-operative tent, another near the receiving tent, another on the evacuation tent. As he shielded the patient, Tanner heard the explosions, felt the terrible jolts of the bombs coming closer and closer. Then the shrapnel ripped into his back.

Within less than a minute it was over. Tanner got to his feet, staggering. The man he covered had not received any further injuries.

"Come on," Tanner said to the other litter-bearer. "Let's get him under shelter, and see who else needs help."

"You need help yourself," the other litter-bearer said. "You're wounded, badly."

"I can wait," Tanner said.

In the 95th Hospital area twenty-six persons had been killed, sixty-four wounded. Most of the tents had been destroyed, including the operating tent.

Here Dr. Howard Patterson of New York had been working on a soldier with a shell fragment in his skull. He and the medics and nurses helping him heard the whine of the bombs. They kept working, until the bomb hit. Two of the nurses fell wounded; the doctor and medics were knocked off their feet by the concussion. When they could stand up they found the tent shredded, operating instruments blown away.

Smoke was still billowing upward when men and nurses from the other hospital units came running to help. The newly wounded were carried to the tents of the 33rd Field Hospital nearby. Other patients were moved to the few tents of the 95th that had not been destroyed. The work went on.

One of the most tragic incidents of that tragic day concerned two soldiers who were not medics. Private Eugene

ABOVE: Rows of ward tents of the 94th Evacuation Hospital, Anzio.
BELOW: The damage is inspected after German shelling at the 56th Evacuation Hospital, Italy.

Mulreaney had been wounded a few days earlier and brought to the hospital. His brother, Private Robert Mulreaney, had come to visit him. Robert was standing beside his brother's cot, talking to him, when he heard the bombs falling. Quickly Robert covered his brother's body with his own. Robert was killed, but he saved his brother's life.

The 95th Evacuation Hospital lost so many of its key personnel in this attack that another unit had to be brought in to relieve it. And on the same day that the 95th was being relieved, the 33rd Field Hospital took a savage pounding of its own.

The attack started with one of those weird incidents that happen in war. About dusk Dr. Chester Dau, a young dentist, was in the admissions tent, looking over a newly arrived patient, when he heard the sudden scream of a shell. Instinctively Dr. Dau and the medic beside him turned their heads and saw, or thought they saw—they could never be sure whether the sight actually registered on their eyes or not—a huge 170-millimeter shell hurtle through the tent, strike the ground a few feet from where they stood, and disappear. Instants later a great cloud of smoke and dust erupted from a hole at their feet. The cloud filled the tent so that for what seemed like hours the men stood blinded, frozen, motionless, waiting for the explosion.

It never came. The shell was a dud.

Other shells followed the first one, and other medics were not so lucky.

Nurse Glenda Spelhaug, who was off duty, was in her tent cooking over a small stove. Nurse LaVerne Farquhar had stopped by to borrow a book. The same shell killed them both.

In the operating tent Dr. James Mason, of Birmingham, Alabama, was preparing a wounded soldier for an operation. Outside the tent a large generator made a humming sound, furnishing electricity for the lights in the operating tent. A shell struck the generator. There was a blinding flash, a terrific concussion that knocked down everyone in the operating tent. Even before they could get to their feet the tent was afire.

Staggering, dazed, acting almost automatically, the doctor and medics got the wounded man off the operating table, onto a litter, and outside the burning tent. Around them shells were still falling. Other tents were afire. A wind was blowing from the nearby mountains, cold and hard. It whipped the fires into leaping, yellow geysers. Tents, half demolished by shells, flapped in the wind, making black shadows against the orange fires.

Through the black and yellow night men and nurses came running. They raced into the burning tents. Using stretchers and cots and mattresses they carried the wounded to safety. Many of the patients had been receiving injections of blood or plasma when the shelling started. Litter-bearers carried them carefully while a nurse or medic walked alongside, holding the needle in the patient's arm with one hand, holding the bottle of blood or plasma with the other.

The shelling stopped as suddenly as it had begun. Whether it had been a deliberate attack on the hospital area or not, no one knew. But the wind still whipped the fires; the medics fought them, searching through the burning tents for more wounded men.

Eventually the fires were put out. New tents were set up. Next day the 33rd Field Hospital was functioning again.

The Anzio hospitals could not possibly hold the steadily increasing number of wounded men. The basic job of the evacuation hospitals and field hospitals was to give quick treatment that would enable a man to return to the front lines, if only slightly wounded, or to be sent by ship to a large general hospital in North Africa, England, or the United States. So each night lines of blacked-out ambulances moved along Purple Heart Alley, the road from the hospital area to the ships in the harbor.

Some of the smaller U.S. naval ships leaving Anzio carried Italian refugees. On one of these Pharmacist's Mate 2nd Class Anthony Savarese was the only corpsman aboard. Savarese spoke some Italian, and it was a good thing, because one of the refugees came rushing up crying that his wife was about to have a baby.

The Navy had not taught Pharmacist's Mate Savarese how to deliver babies. This was not expected to be a routine duty for a corpsman. But something had to be done. And

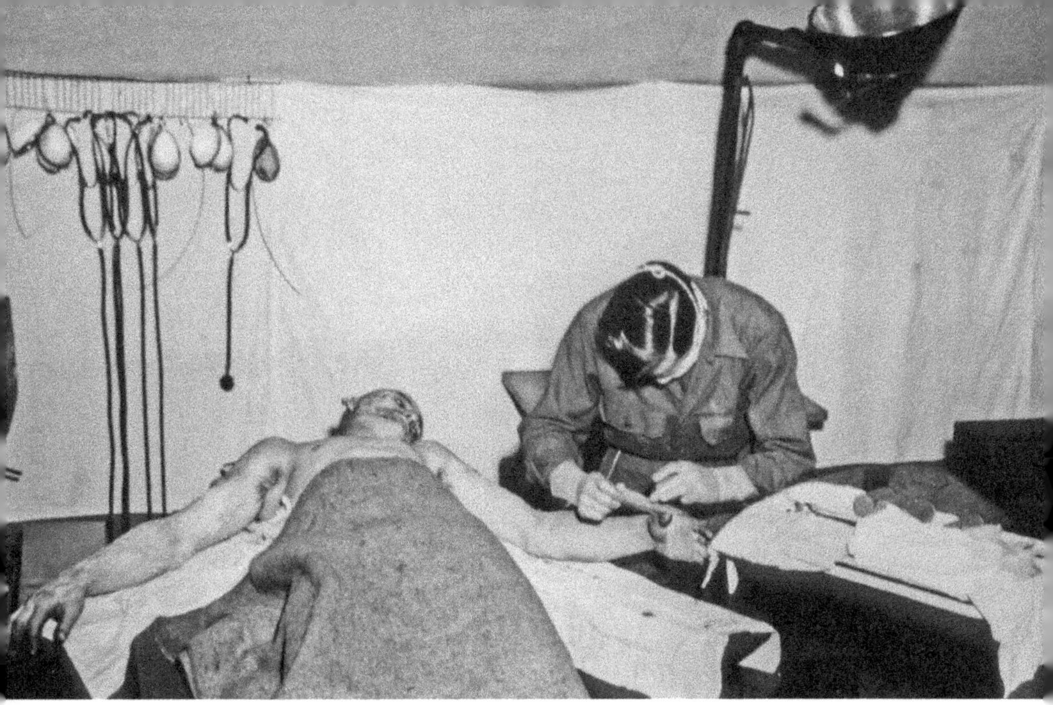

A medic dresses the burned arm of a patient in the surgery tent of the 94th Evacuation Hospital, Anzio.

with the help of one of the ship's officers, Savarese safely delivered the baby.

The ship's crew took up a collection to help the baby's parents, whose home had been destroyed in the fighting. The two Navy crewmen who gave the most were George Milan and Raymond Devlin. So Mr. and Mrs. Camili named their new baby George Raymond Camili.

As the Anzio winter turned into spring, the weather grew slightly drier. Army engineers drained part of the nearby swamp, and the foxholes could be dug deeper than before without turning into swimming pools. As day followed day the medics filled more and more sandbags and stacked them around the walls of their tents. Eventually the whole hospital area except the roofs appeared to be buried. But still there was no protection from a direct hit by bomb or shell.

In Charleston, South Carolina, Army medics prepare to unload wounded men from Italy and North Africa brought by U.S. Army Hospital Ship *Acadia*. Rows and rows of stretchers lie in readiness.

And the Germans kept on bombing and shelling. Shells from "Whistling Willie" and "Anzio Annie"—as the Americans had nicknamed the big German guns in the hills—made a thin wailing sound, far worse on the nerves than the whine of a falling bomb. The listening medics learned to distinguish their own shells from those of the Germans. They could tell the sound of a gun from the sound of an ammunition dump exploding. They could distinguish the sounds of the British planes and those of the Germans. More than once a man's life depended on this kind of knowledge.

All this time more Allied troops were being sent into the area. Finally in late May the Americans and British unleashed an attack that broke the German lines. The Allied Army moved rapidly northward. As they went, the medics went with them. But no man who had been at Anzio would ever forget it.

D-DAY
CHAPTER SEVEN

Even before the United States entered World War II, German armies had invaded and conquered France. They stood poised on the edge of the English Channel. For a long time they seemed likely to invade England.

After the Japanese bombed Pearl Harbor, American soldiers were sent not only to the Pacific, but also to England to help the British in their fight against the Germans. American planes flew from English airfields to bomb Germany. And plans were made for American and British armies to cross the English Channel, land in France, and drive through France against Germany.

The landing on the coast of Normandy would be the greatest amphibious operation in all history up to that time. The Germans had turned the French coast into one vast fortress. Everyone knew that casualties would be heavy. The Medical Departments of the U.S. Army and the U.S. Navy began to prepare careful plans.

Hospitals had to be built in England. Some of these were permanent buildings of brick and stone. Some were only huge tents or groups of tents; but they were stocked with the best of medical supplies. Warehouses had to be built to hold reserve equipment, and each warehouse was furnished with approximately 2,000 different items. The Navy prepared to ship more than 7,000 surgical-knife blades every year, more than 32,000 hypodermic needles, 370,000 yards of gauze for dressings, four tons of absorbent cotton.

There were plans for where and how the doctors and medics would reach the wounded men, and how these wounded would be brought from the French coast to England.

The plan here was basically similar to the one used at Anzio, but on a much greater scale. Teams of doctors and medics would go ashore with the infantry. Aid stations would be set up back of sand dunes or houses or wherever there was some slight shelter. Litter-bearers would bring the seriously wounded to the aid stations for brief, emergency treatment: a bandage, a tourniquet, a shot of morphine

Casualties, given first aid on the battlefield, are transported by jeep to clearing stations behind the lines for further treatment.

to dull the pain. A tag would be placed on the wounded man to show what had been done. Then he would be taken, usually in a jeep designed to carry two, three, or four litters to a collecting or clearing station.

All this time boats would be bringing more men and supplies ashore. Some of these would be LSTs (landing ship, tank), shallow-draft ships built to carry tanks, trucks, and heavy equipment into combat. Sometimes these could run directly onto the beach to unload. When they did, then the wounded could be placed directly on board. When it was necessary for the LSTs to lay a short distance offshore, the wounded would be carried to them in small boats. Then the LSTs would take them back to England.

Not all the invading troops, however, were carried across the Channel in ships. Long before dawn on D-Day, June 6, 1944, transport planes as well as bombers and fighters were lifting off British airfields into the night sky, heading for France. In the transports were paratroopers to be dropped behind the German lines. And with the paratroops went Army doctors and medics.

One of the medics was Sergeant Charles Short. At two o'clock in the morning his plane was crossing the French coast. Antiaircraft fire came up to meet it. As the plane bored inland, the fire grew heavier. In the dark plane the paratroopers, heavy with guns and ammunition, stood waiting for the order to jump.

Sergeant Short carried no guns or ammunition. Strapped to his legs were two first-aid kits. In big canvas pockets he carried light splints for repairing broken bones.

Heavily laden paratroopers on D-Day, flying toward Normandy to jump before dawn.

His uniform bulged with packaged bandages, sulfa for disinfecting wounds, scissors, plasma, morphine. But he had nothing to protect him against the enemy below.

Then came the order to jump. Sergeant Short stepped out into the cold blast of night air. He felt himself falling through darkness, then the shock of the parachute opening. He could not see the ground below and he tried not to look for it. Just wait, he told himself, and keep relaxed. He hoped he would not come down in a tree or on a German gun emplacement. There was no firing beneath him. Overhead, the plane had gone. Everything was quiet.

He landed in a ditch beside a narrow, dirt road. Quickly he reefed in his parachute and cut himself free. In the darkness he could see no sign of the men who had jumped with him. Cautiously he began to move down the road.

Ahead of him a dark figure arose from beside the road. Before Short could speak a voice challenged him—in English. It was one of the paratroopers, and Short answered with the password.

A few minutes later they joined up with more paratroopers. But nobody knew where they were. For days they had studied maps of the area in which they were to land; but something had gone wrong. This was not the right place.

Off toward the coast, they could hear guns firing. So they walked that way. The firing became more general. Soon it seemed to come from all sides. And now the sky was turning gray with dawn.

It was about this time that Short found a soldier lying beside the road. He was an American and had been hit in the chest by machine-gun fire. When Short examined the wound, he was certain the man could not live. But during his training he had been taught never to give up. Carefully he applied a battle dressing. He inserted a needle into the man's arm and knelt beside him, holding the bottle while plasma seeped into his vein.

It was daylight now. From somewhere close ahead Short could hear the rattle of machine-gun fire, the deeper boom of a mortar. The paratroopers had moved on to join the fighting. Short and the wounded man were alone.

Short knew the man could not survive being put over his shoulder and carried. Besides, there was no place to carry him. But Short knew also that with the fighting close ahead there would be more wounded, and more work for him. He made the man as comfortable as possible and left him beside the road.

Later that morning Sergeant Short found an aid station and told the litter-bearers where he had left the wounded man. But in the hours that followed there was no chance to learn if the litter-bearers found him, or if he was still alive.

Several months later, back in England, Sergeant Short saw a soldier on the street who looked familiar. He kept staring at the man—and all at once he knew: it was the same soldier he had found beside the road in France. Here he was, completely recovered.

While Sergeant Short was swinging in his parachute over France, Pharmacist's Mate 1st Class Sam Schiek was eating a predawn breakfast on an LST in the English

Channel. It was quite a breakfast: steak and ice cream. Everybody on board tried to eat, no matter how nervous his stomach muscles. No one could be sure that he would live to have another meal.

The daylight came gradually. As the sky lightened, Schiek could see ships in front, behind, and on both sides, as far as the eye could reach. Ships of all sizes and shapes, so close together they were in constant danger of collision, were heading for the coast of France. Overhead planes were passing, flight after flight, filling the sky.

With dawn Schiek began to hear the gunfire. The LST passed great battleships that moved slowly, parallel to the coast, and hurled their 16-inch projectiles over the tops of other ships to pound the beach and the fortifications behind it. Closer to shore were cruisers, and nearer still destroyers, firing so steadily that the sound drowned out the roar of airplane engines overhead.

Closest in, a swarm of small boats raced back and forth carrying men and supplies to the beach. German shells burst among them, throwing great geysers of water into the air. Through it all the LST moved in to drop its ramp close to shore. From its bow the tanks rumbled through shallow water toward the beach.

Even while the tanks were being unloaded, the corpsmen and the crew were converting the LST into a hospital ship. The decks were scrubbed, disinfected. Cots were put up to hold the wounded. Brackets along the bulkheads were lowered to hold triple-deck beds.

Around them the German shells continued to fall. Sam

Schiek was working on the tank deck when suddenly it reeled and leaped beneath him. The LST had taken a direct hit near the stern. But damage was slight, and work continued. Days later Schiek would write to his mother:

> There was utter confusion. The ship next to us had been hit hard. There were people dying and being wounded. Ten of us were told to get in a small boat and go over, amidst the shelling, and patch them up. I tried to make my knees quit knocking, but couldn't. We were lowering the first-aid trunk into the small boat when another salvo of shells struck. I hit the deck so hard I almost went through it. The Doc and I cracked skulls. My helmet came off. Going down the ladder I heard another shell coming and I let go and dropped into the boat.
>
> There was the car-ump-boom! of shells all around us. We made for the port side of the stricken ship. But there was no ladder and we had to turn around and head for the bow doors which were open. We never reached there. We got stuck on a sandbar and had to wade, waist-deep in water. Three of us were carrying the first-aid trunk. The soldiers on shore had put up a smoke screen and for a few minutes it was so thick we couldn't see where we were. In the confusion, we wound up on the beach.

The beach was being lashed by machine-gun and artillery fire. Schiek and the other corpsmen began to stumble along it, carrying the heavy trunk. By this time part of the smoke had blown away. Bullets whipped past. A shell burst close to one side. Ahead of them a shellhole offered some protection. But in the sand, burdened by the heavy trunk, the corpsmen could not move rapidly.

"Give me that crate," Schiek said. He was five feet nine, slender, and not particularly strong. But he swung the

On the Normandy beachhead, Allied troops prepare to move forward. In the background, medics assist those wounded in their first few minutes ashore.

trunk onto his shoulder and ran, sand flying, to dive headlong into the shellhole, his friends close after him.

There was a pause in the firing. When Schiek raised his head he saw a soldier crouching back of a sand dune a hundred feet away.

"You medics!" the soldier shouted. "Don't try to move! You're in a minefield!"

"I took his word for it," Schiek wrote to his mother. "I stayed right where I was until they got a path through the mines. Then I tried to pick up the aid trunk and carry it out. I couldn't budge it. Now it took all three of us to drag it."

By the time Schiek reached his own ship again, it was ready to turn back toward England. But there was no chance for the corpsmen to rest. Wounded men were everywhere. Beds filled the big deck where the tanks had been, and every bed was taken. Walking wounded, men with heads or arms or feet bandaged, filled the top deck. Some stood looking back toward the beach. Others sat on the deck with their backs against the bulkhead. Others lay stretched out, too exhausted to move. Over them all was an almost eerie silence. They did not talk; they did not complain. Even the wounded on the cots, many of them unconscious, rarely moaned with pain. They lay patient, quiet, waiting.

There were approximately four hundred wounded men on this LST. To take care of them there were twenty-four corpsmen and one doctor. In the ship's sickbay, an operating room now, the doctor and several corpsmen worked steadily on the more desperate cases. On the tank deck the corpsmen moved from bed to bed, changing bandages, giving morphine and plasma.

It was night and the LST sailed without lights. In the darkness, all around it, were other ships, some heading for France, others returning. Overhead there was an almost steady roar of passing planes. But the working corpsmen had no way of knowing if the planes were Allied or German —unless they heard a bomb fall.

Then for the second time in twenty-four hours Pharmacist's Mate Schiek got orders to leave his ship and go to another in distress. This one had struck a mine. Like many of the LSTs it had no doctor aboard, only corpsmen. Many of the corpsmen had been injured. Help was needed. Once more Schiek went over the side of his own LST and

ABOVE: In this iconic photo, *Into the Jaws of Death*, troops wade ashore after leaving their LCVP (landing craft, vehicle, personnel) to join the D-Day battle.
BELOW: LCMs (landing craft, mechanized) become rescue ships for the casualties, with the men being transferred to a larger ship for evacuation from Normandy.

down the ship's ladder. The sea was rough. The small boat below rose high with a wave, then shot downward, almost disappearing in the darkness. And rose again. When it reached its crest, close below him, Schiek jumped. He fell hard, but unhurt. Other corpsmen followed.

The mined ship was close by, wallowing slowly in the rough sea. As Schiek climbed aboard he kept wondering if it were about to sink, and kept trying to put the thought out of his mind. Then he was on board, had passed through the blackout doors—and there was no longer time to think of what might happen if the ship went down.

The place was a shambles. The explosion of the mine had hurled the wounded men's cots into the air like straws in a storm. Among the wreckage men lay sprawled in strange positions. Wounded men had been injured again. Corpsmen who had been standing on the deck, tending the wounded when the explosion occurred, had had their ankles broken. Now, unable to walk, they crawled among the wounded, giving first aid.

It was a nightmare that Schiek was never able to remember very clearly. He lost track of time. It had been night, then it was day, and then night again. He could not remember when he had slept or eaten. At some point a doctor came aboard to help with the work. Eventually—it was day again now—the crippled ship moved into an English harbor. The wounded were sent ashore. And Schiek went to sleep. Next day he rejoined his own ship and headed once more toward France.

GERMANY'S WESTERN FRONT
CHAPTER EIGHT

It was D-Day plus three. The 2nd Regiment of the 29th Infantry Division was moving cautiously through the Normandy village of Colombières. The Germans had retreated, but they had left behind snipers to pick off the unwary.

Dr. Roger Watson and Dr. Elmer Carter rode in a Medical Department jeep. Both men knew that sitting there in the open they made a fine target for the snipers. But the jeep was plainly marked with Red Crosses, a Red Cross flag flew beside the wind shield, and the doctors wore Red Crosses on their helmets and sleeves. In North Africa and Italy, before the invasion of Normandy, the Germans had usually respected the Red Cross symbol. But not always. No one could be sure.

Near the middle of the village a French civilian came running from one of the houses. In French he called, "Are you doctors?"

Dr. Watson, who spoke French, answered him. "We are."

"Please," the Frenchman said. "My two children were injured yesterday when the village was shelled. There is no doctor here. Will you help?"

Watson and Carter looked at each other. Their unit was moving on. The war was not going to wait for wounded

A Medical Corps jeep accompanies American troops moving through Carentan, France, the first French city to fall to the invaders. June 17, 1944

children. But Dr. Carter, who was the senior officer, said, "Go with him, Roger. I'll move on with the outfit. You can catch up with us."

Watson took one medic with him. They found the children, a boy and girl, in a shed. Neither was badly wounded. The doctor bandaged their wounds and was about to leave when another Frenchman came in. A half-mile beyond the village, he said, was an old man, badly hurt. Would the doctor come to him?

Dr. Carter had gone ahead with the jeep. Now Watson and his aid man rode with the Frenchman in a horse-drawn cart. They carried a Red Cross flag. In the distance they could hear firing, but no soldiers were in sight.

The old man was lying in bed in a small cottage. A shell fragment had ripped a long gap in his thigh. Some of the torn flesh had to be cut away, the steel fragment removed, the wound sterilized. As Dr. Watson worked his back was to the cottage door. His medic was on the other side of the bed, facing the door and a window.

Suddenly the medic said, "Oh, oh!" His voice sounded strangled.

A German nurse and U.S. Army medic help each other while treating a German soldier in Unna, Germany.

Intent on his work. Dr. Watson did not look up.

The medic whispered, "Doc, here come some Germans! Eight of 'em!"

There was no time and no place to hide. Watson's hands never stopped their work, but in the same instant he was wondering if he would be shot, taken prisoner, or what. Behind him he heard the cottage door open. He could feel the eyes of the Germans on his back like a physical touch. Later Dr. Watson would tell Dr. Carter, "As an intern, I sometimes tried to impress the nurses by pretending not to care when things went horribly wrong in the operating room. So I tried the same trick on the Germans. In fact, there wasn't anything else I could do."

To his aid man he said casually, "They probably saw the Red Cross flag we left at the door and won't bother us. So let's get on with our work."

Trying to keep his hands steady, Watson finished suturing the wound. He never looked around. He began to put on the bandage. It was very quiet in the room. At last he heard the sound of the door closing.

The medic ran to the window. "They're leaving, Doc! They just stood there, with their rifles in their hands, staring at us. And then they walked off."

At this point Dr. Watson's hands began to tremble. He could not stop them, and for a few moments he had to quit trying to tie the bandage.

Later Watson would learn of times when American and German medics actually helped one another. On one occasion a German medic, wearing Red Cross armbands, drove a haycart straight through the American lines. Not a shot was fired at him, not even before the Americans learned that in the cart were three wounded soldiers: two Germans and an American. The German explained that his own soldiers had retreated. Since he had no way to take care of the wounded, he was trying to get them to an American hospital.

Unfortunately, things did not always work out this way. An arm band was no protection against artillery or mortar fire. And there were some Germans who deliberately shot at medics. Dr. Elmer Carter, Watson's friend, was killed by small-arms fire just nine days after Watson had been left unmolested by the German soldiers.

Like Dr. Watson, Dr. John Richter of La Porte, Indiana, had gone into the Army almost directly from medical school. In the invasion of France he served as a battalion surgeon with a tank outfit. His job was to follow so closely on the heels of the tanks that he could quickly rescue the wounded men from any tank knocked out by mines or shellfire. To help him, he had four medics and an armored half-track—a vehicle somewhat like a small tank but without guns and converted into a kind of ambulance.

In theory Dr. Richter might have stayed some distance back of the tanks and sent his aid men forward to bring back the wounded. Doctors were too few and too valuable to be risked more than necessary. But young Dr. Richter felt responsible for the work of his medics, and he knew their training had been limited. So whenever one of his aid men was sent forward for the first time, Richter went with him.

ABOVE: A wounded American soldier is loaded into an M-3 half-track in Echtz, Germany, 1944.
BELOW: An armored M-3 half-track converted for ambulance duty.

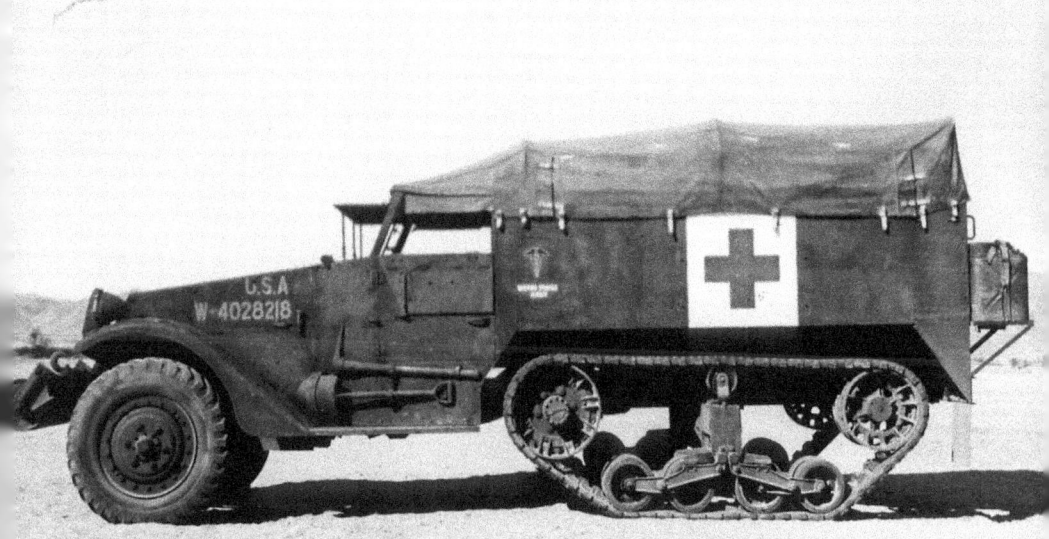

This was why, when the radio call came saying that one of the tanks had been knocked out by artillery fire and the tank commander wounded, Richter jumped into his half-track with the driver and raced forward.

This part of France was a region of small fields surrounded by hedges. The tank was in a field, still smoldering, and looking like some huge, crippled animal. All along the hedgerow, only fifty feet away, American infantrymen were dug in. From another hedgerow, Germans raked the field with small-arms fire. And from somewhere out of sight, the big gun that had knocked out the tank was still firing. Richter's half-track drove up alongside the tank. Quickly he and the aid man leaped out and climbed onto the smoldering tank. The turret was open. Richter climbed inside. The heat was almost unbearable. He found the tank commander sprawled unconscious, and carefully lifted him to where the medic above could pull him out. Moments later they had him inside the half-track ambulance.

All around them rifles and machine guns were firing. A bullet struck the tank and ricocheted past Richter's head. From the corner of his eye, he saw one of the American infantrymen near the hedge spin and fall.

Richter ran toward the fallen soldier, his aid man following with a stretcher. The soldier had been shot through the throat, but he was still alive. Swiftly Richter and the medic rolled him onto the stretcher and ran back to put him in the half-track. Richter climbed in beside the wounded man. The aid man jumped into the driver's seat and sent the half-track lumbering across the field.

The bullet, Dr. Richter saw, had passed through the soldier's throat, cutting the trachea and several large blood vessels. The man was bleeding badly. The harsh, gasping breath came through the hole in the trachea, making bloody bubbles.

The half-track turned out of the field down a narrow lane. It was rough going. The vehicle rolled and pitched like a small boat in a storm. Bracing himself the best he could, using the two hemostats from his aid kit, Dr. Richter managed to clamp off the bleeding veins. But already blood and air inside the man's throat was causing it to swell, cutting off his breath. In a few more minutes he would choke to death.

The half-track rolled up to the aid station and stopped. Dr. Richter shouted for his tracheotomy set, and a medic came running. With a scalpel, Richter slashed at the wounded man's throat. He pushed his finger into the incision, thinking: My finger's dirty, filthy, but there's no time to scrub; I'll just have to pray there's no infection.

He found the hole in the trachea, then pushed a tube into it and down the soldier's throat. Now he could breathe through the tube, and Richter quickly began artificial respiration.

The soldier coughed violently, blowing a mass of blood out of the tube. Richter kept on with the artificial respiration. Within minutes the soldier was breathing on his own, and Richter could turn his attention to the tank commander, who was less seriously wounded.

Captain Garland Adamson, M.D., the 761st "Black Panthers" Tank Battalion's medical officer. During a battle in France, Captain Adamson proceeded on foot through artillery barrage from the aid station to wounded men, saving several lives with total disregard for his own personal safety, earning a Bronze Star. At age 50, he was the oldest member of the battalion.

Later Dr. John Richter was awarded a Silver Star. It was not for this action alone, however. The award also read:

On another occasion he went approximately 300 yards beyond the furthest friendly troops to evacuate an injured soldier. In the race across France he followed directly in the wake of the advancing tanks, rendering expert medical care to the wounded, directing and encouraging the activities of his own aid men, and was constantly exposed to sniper, machine-gun, and mortar fire. At Fossieux Ridge in the midst of an all-enveloping fog which impeded the evacuation of casualties, Captain Richter went forward and rendered aid to numerous wounded soldiers. On innumerable occasions he visited advance tank positions where enemy fire was so intense that the tank crews could not leave the comparative safety of their vehicles. These instances cited are not isolated cases where Captain Richter placed the welfare of the wounded above the risk of his own life, but are merely a few of the many deeds which exemplify his courage, skill, fortitude, and zealous devotion to duty....

Through all this Dr. Richter was never injured. Not all doctors were as lucky. Dr. Moses Rabson, of Philadelphia, got the Purple Heart Medal for being wounded, to add to his Bronze and Silver Star Medals for heroism. It happened this way.

Dr. Rabson's armored reconnaissance battalion was fighting near the city of Mons in Belgium. Dr. Rabson, who had already been awarded a Bronze Star for heroism, had set up his aid station behind a low hill. He was here when an American self-propelled howitzer lumbered past. It went up the hill, over the crest, and moments later there was a deafening explosion. The howitzer had been hit by an antitank gun.

As the sound of the explosion faded, Rabson could hear a man screaming in pain.

At this time Dr. Rabson was alone in the aid station. He grabbed an aid kit and began to run. At first the hill itself gave some protection; then he was on the crest, completely exposed to German fire. The crippled howitzer was thirty yards away. Beyond it, in the valley below, Rabson could see the flash of German guns firing at him.

Running hard, Rabson reached the howitzer and climbed on top. The turret was open. Looking inside, the doctor saw a soldier staring up at him.

"I can't get out!" the man cried.

"Give me your hands."

Somehow Rabson lifted the soldier out of the turret onto the deck. As he did so, he saw that the man's left leg hung only by a tendon; the lower half was turning slowly like something on the end of a string. It would be difficult to carry the man under any circumstances; in this condition it was almost impossible. Swiftly—he could never remember just what he said—the doctor explained that it would be impossible to save the leg.

"All right," the soldier said. "Take it off."

Using a pair of scissors from his aid kit, Rabson cut the tendon. The leg fell clear. Rabson leaped down, took the wounded man in his arms, and began to run. Shells were bursting around them. Staggering, Rabson ran toward a clump of bushes that offered some slight protection. Then he fell, unable to carry the man any farther.

From somewhere a soldier appeared. The doctor had never seen him before, would never see him again. He said, "I'll help you, Doc," and together they got the wounded man over the hill to the aid station. Swiftly Rabson set to work to stop the bleeding.

(Three years later, after the war was over. Dr. Moses Rabson was doing postgraduate work in orthopedic surgery at a Veterans Clinic in New York. A veteran came in to be fitted for an artificial leg. He and Dr. Rabson got to talking—and the soldier turned out to be the same one Rabson had pulled from the howitzer.)

In rescuing this soldier, Dr. Rabson was uninjured. Exactly two weeks later his luck changed.

Now his battalion was in Germany, fighting its way through a village. A radio call came to the aid station that men had been wounded just beyond a street corner. With one medic, Rabson set out to answer the call. They rode in a half-track ambulance with Red Crosses four feet high painted on the sides. Both the doctor and aid man had Red Crosses on their helmets and their sleeves.

The half-track turned the corner where the wounded men were supposed to be. Everything was quiet, with not a person in sight. Dr. Rabson got out of the ambulance to look for the wounded.

A machine gun opened fire. Bullets ricocheted wildly off the half-track. One struck Dr. Rabson in the side, knocking him down. He rolled over, shouting for the driver to back the half-track around the corner out of fire. Then he crawled after it.

Next day at a field hospital. Dr. Rabson was operated on. The bullet had passed cleanly through his side without doing serious damage. Five days later the wound was still painfully sore, but Rabson felt he was well enough to rejoin his outfit. When the other doctors did not agree, Rabson strolled casually out of the hospital, hitched a ride in a passing jeep, and went back to his unit.

Even in the toughest fighting the American soldier's sense of humor often kept him going. Dr. Frank England of Mobile, Alabama, was leaning over a wounded man, about to give a shot of morphine when the man said weakly, "Doc, I'm already full of holes. Do you have to punch another one in me?"

Dr. England and Clay Combe, one of his aid men, had a private joke of their own that lasted through much of the war. While in training in the United States, Combe had fainted at his first sight of blood while helping the doctor lance a boil on a soldier's arm. But in France and Germany, Combe went time and again into combat to bring back desperately wounded and mangled men. Each time he returned to the aid station, England would ask, "Clay, did you faint?"

And Combe would say, "Not this time. Doc. But I was mighty dizzy there for awhile."

On one occasion Combe was driving Dr. England in a

scout car when it ran over a mine. The explosion hurled the doctor against the roof and then out of the car. For several moments he staggered about, dazed, not sure where he was. Then he saw Combe lying on the ground beside the wrecked car. As England leaned over him, Combe opened his eyes, blinked, and said, "Hey, Doc, you're wounded. Lie down here while I bandage your head."

They bandaged each other's wounds. Later England would write to his wife that x-rays showed his skull was not fractured. "But now," he wrote, "I have a fine excuse if I ever forget your birthday or anniversary or something of that sort. I'll just blame it on this bang I got on the head when we ran over the mine."

Mines were among the most deadly and frightening of all weapons. They were hidden under roads and paths, sometimes hidden by the hundreds across entire fields. It took a special, cold courage to move in a mined area. It was the kind of courage the unarmed medics had to have.

In the attack on Germany's Siegfried Line in March 1945, Private Fred Murphy, a medic from Weymouth, Massachusetts, went ahead with the first wave of infantry. They were met by intense machine-gun, mortar, and artillery fire. A machine-gun bullet struck Murphy in the right shoulder. It was not a critical wound, but it bled freely and most men would have turned back. Instead, Murphy stuffed a battle dressing against his wound and moved on, taking care of other wounded, giving first aid, calling for litter-bearers to carry the men to the rear while he went forward with the fighting.

At this point his unit ran into a large minefield. Quickly a half-dozen men went down, killed or wounded. How many mines there were in the field, no one knew. But there was no way at this point to clear them, and the only way to reach the wounded men was to go into the field.

Private Fred Murphy went. He knew that any step might be his last. There was no way of knowing where the mines might be hidden. It was simply a matter of blind chance. Private Murphy walked straight into the field, to a man whose foot had been blown off. He applied a tourniquet, gave morphine, picked the man up in his arms and walked back out of the field.

He could have stopped there. His own wound was bleeding again. Instead he went back into the minefield. He did not try to dodge because there was no way of knowing where or how to dodge. He reached another wounded man and brought him out.

And went back again.

It could not last. Murphy stepped on a mine that blew off one foot. And still he did not turn back. He was crawling, still trying to save another life, when he struck the mine that killed him. Posthumously he was awarded the Congressional Medal of Honor, the nation's highest decoration for courage and devotion to duty.

Engineers from a U.S. Army Mine Platoon prepare to sweep the road for enemy mines in war-torn Stockheim, Germany, 1945.

ARMY AND NAVY MEDICS AT SEA
CHAPTER NINE

While the Allied armies fought their way across Europe, it was the Navy's job to keep them supplied as well as to carry on its part of the war in the Pacific. Huge convoys moved steadily back and forth across the Atlantic. Sometimes there were vicious battles with German submarines; but on many voyages nothing at all happened. For the doctors and corpsmen on board, life sometimes seemed more drudgery than excitement.

Hospital Corpsman Bentz Plagemann later wrote to a friend describing how time was spent on board a destroyer.

Our bandages and dressings did not come to us already prepared. We made them. Almost every afternoon while on convoy duty in the Atlantic, we corpsmen sat in sick bay with our needles and thread and scissors. We made the surgical masks for use in an operation. We made the glove cases in which the rubber gloves for operating were put. We folded the gauze squares, or "sponges," used in operating, and were taught to fold the gauze so that all cut edges would be inside, and no loose thread could get in an incision.

We even made our own pills. We did not even have aspirin tablets aboard. Instead, the powders were mixed with a sort of spatula on a metal surface. We filled the capsules by pressing the two empty halves into the powder, and then pressing the halves together.

One afternoon Plagemann's destroyer received orders to sail at dawn the next day on convoy duty. Supplies were hurriedly brought on board. Among them was a fifty-yard bolt of cloth for the medical department. The corpsmen were supposed to make the cloth into fifty towels. Each towel would have to be double-hemmed at both ends so that when they were used in operating or in dressing a wound, no loose thread could get into the wound. It was going to be a long, hard job with needle and thread.

Young Plagemann looked unhappily at the huge bolt of cloth. And then he had an idea.

On the dock near the destroyer was a telephone. Plagemann went to the phone and called the home of the admiral who commanded the naval base. He asked for the admiral's wife and explained the situation.

"Please," he said, "isn't there some group of Navy wives who can help us with all this sewing?"

The admiral's wife may have been somewhat surprised at the request. Nobody had asked her such a thing before. But it took her only a few seconds to recover.

"Of course we'll help," she said. "I'll send a car to pick up the cloth right away."

So all that night a group of officers' wives sat somewhere sewing hard. And next morning just before dawn, the fifty towels, beautifully hemmed, were delivered. The destroyer sailed. And Plagemann was the hero of its medical department.

Three hospital ships docked in Yokohama, Japan: *Tjitjalengka* (British), *Marigold* (U.S. Army), and *Benevolence* (U.S. Navy), to bring home prisoners of war held by the Japanese. August/September 1945

Often the hours of training and getting ready seemed boring, but when tragedy struck they paid off. Probably no ship in the fleet illustrated this better than the light cruiser *Birmingham*, operating in the Pacific.

In November 1943 the *Birmingham* was hit by a torpedo. There were only a few casualties, but the episode made the medical department more aware than ever of the need for intensive training. So day after day, month after month, the lectures and practice continued. Then in October 1944 in the Battle for Leyte Gulf the carrier *Princeton* was hit by one of the Japanese *kamikazes*. These were planes flown by pilots determined to commit suicide by crashing their aircraft into American ships. Great fires were started, and the *Birmingham* went close alongside to help fight the fires. To do this, a great many of the *Birmingham's* crew had to be on their ship's exposed deck.

Suddenly the *Princeton* was shattered by a terrific explosion. Pieces of the carrier, some as big as houses, were hurled high in the air—before crashing down on the cruiser. Within seconds 229 of the *Birmingham's* crew were killed and 420 wounded. In the long hours and days that followed, the doctors and corpsmen of the *Birmingham* worked without stopping, worked until they were staggering from exhaustion—and kept working.

Even so, there were simply not enough doctors and corpsmen to take care of the wounded. Untrained members of the crew had to be brought in to help. And when it was all over—the wounded finally ashore in hospitals, the *Birmingham* repaired and at sea once more—the ship's doctors started a new training program. This included not only the corpsmen, but most of the crew. Everyone had to be able to give first aid if necessary.

It would prove necessary, in what was probably the worst tragedy ever to befall a ship's medical department. Six months after the Battle for Leyte Gulf, the *Birmingham* was in action off Okinawa. A Japanese suicide plane, carrying a 500-pound bomb, came out of the sun. The *Birmingham's* guns threw up a wall of fire. But the plane dived through it and struck the ship's Number 2 turret. The bomb tore free, ripped through three decks, and exploded near the sick bay. Both the ship's doctors were killed and nineteen of the twenty-four corpsmen were killed or wounded, along with many of the crew.

Pharmacist's Mate Henry Collins was one of the five corpsmen uninjured. Later he would say: "I don't know how we got through the first hour. We couldn't have, if it hadn't been for the training given to the crew. Men who had never put a bandage on a real wound took care of horrible injuries. And corpsmen left their own wounds untended to look after others. After awhile doctors and corpsmen from other ships came to help. But there were lives saved that day by men who a month before had griped about learning to tie a tourniquet."

Sometimes tragedy struck a ship with no warning, not even the call to battle stations. This was what happened to the *Cape San Juan*, an Army transport carrying some 1500 troops from the United States to Australia.

Captain John Shurts of Eldora, Iowa, was the only doctor on board. He had twelve aid men, but as day after day passed peacefully they had no work to do except treat an occasional cold.

Then came the morning of November 10, 1943. It was a gray dawn, with wind and rain. The South Pacific rolled in long, slow swells. At 0530 (5:30 a.m.) Dr. Shurts was asleep in his bunk when something lifted him and threw him against the overhead. He fell back, rolled off the bunk onto the deck, then staggered to his feet. It took him a few moments to realize that the *Cape San Juan* had been torpedoed.

The torpedo had struck alongside the Number 3 hold in which troops were sleeping. Many had been killed, many more wounded. Shurts and his aid men went to work.

The wounded men had to be brought from the flooded hold to sick bay. Soon they filled the beds and were stretched on the deck. There were emergency first-aid dressings to be applied, and artificial respiration, plasma, morphine to be given. Doctor and aid men worked furiously —but in the back of their minds they all knew that the ship was sinking. And their job was with the wounded men, far below decks.

Finally came the order to abandon ship.

One by one, Dr. Shurts and his aid men brought the casualties topside. Already lifeboats and rafts had been lowered. But there were not enough to take care of all the men. Many swam, wearing life jackets. Shurts got all the wounded he could into lifeboats. When there was no room for any more, he stayed with the others on the *Cape San Juan*.

Two American seaplanes arrived and began to circle the area. Occasionally they landed and picked up an exhausted swimmer. But they had room for only a few, and they could not take the casualties aboard. The *Cape San Juan* sank lower in the sea.

An American freighter came over the horizon. Pulling close, it lowered its own boats and sent them alongside the *Cape San Juan*. Dr. Shurts got the last of his wounded men into the boats. Then he too went over the side of the sinking ship.

A few minutes later he was headed back for it again. He had learned that the rescue vessel had very little in the way of medical supplies. He did not want to ask someone else to return to the sinking ship, so he went himself. He climbed on board—it wasn't much of a climb now, since the rail was almost under water—and fought his way up the slanting deck. Then he went below. He knew that if the ship sank now he would be trapped. But there were wounded men who needed help and he had to have supplies.

He got them. He climbed back up the ladders to the deck, slid down the deck to the rail, and passed the supplies to the waiting lifeboat. Then he went over the side himself.

A few minutes later the *Cape San Juan* slid beneath the surface. Dr. John Shurts did not have time to watch it. On the rescue vessel, he and his aid men were already at work among the wounded.

Another doctor who was among the last to leave a sinking ship was Captain W. D. Davis, the senior medical officer on the carrier *Yorktown* at the Battle of Midway in June 1942. In fact, Dr. Davis and his assistant, Dr. French, were almost left on board by mistake. They were in an operating room, working over a wounded sailor, when the order was given to abandon ship. Intent on their work, neither of them heard the order. They went on with their operation. When they had finished and the patient was bandaged and ready to be removed to sick bay, Dr. Davis stepped out into the corridor and called for a corpsman. Nobody answered him. No one was in sight. Even the sick bay was empty.

"Corpsman!" Davis shouted. "Corpsman!"

This time he got an answer. A man came running down an alleyway. "We've been ordered to abandon ship, Doctor, a long time ago! I was making a last check!"

"I'm glad of that," Davis said. "Come on."

Dr. Davis, the corpsman, and Dr. French lifted the unconscious patient and began to carry him topside. It was not easy carrying him down the long alleyways, up the steep ladders. But they got the man on deck and lowered him over the side onto one of the last rafts. Dr. French and the corpsman followed.

Dr. Davis was aware the great ship might go down at any moment. But in the back of his mind was the fear that some of his corpsmen or some of the wounded might still be below. After all, he and Dr. French had not heard the order. There might be others. So once more he went below, this time all alone. Down the ladders, down the long corridors, deeper and deeper into the ship. He kept calling as he went, and there was only the echo of his own voice. His search was fast but thorough. When he was absolutely sure that no one had been left, he climbed again to the flight deck.

Now the flight deck was empty. Along the entire length of the ship, Davis could not see a single person. He felt sure he was the last man on board. (Actually, he was not. The ship's captain, true to the tradition of the sea, was making his own last search to be sure no one was left.)

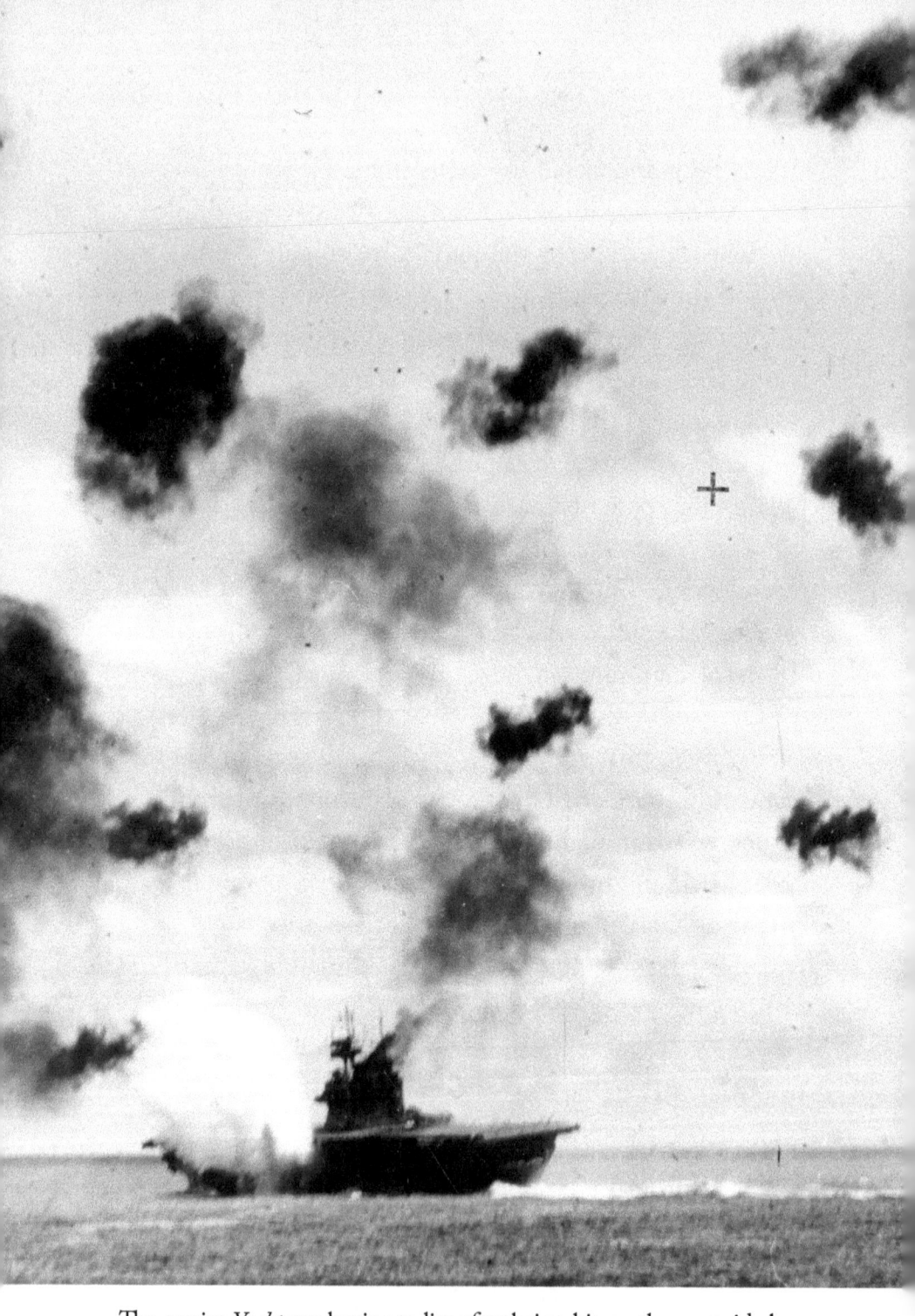

The carrier *Yorktown* begins to list after being hit on the port side by a Japanese Type 91 aerial torpedo in the Battle of Midway. Note very heavy antiaircraft fire. The "+" is the camera aiming cross.

In the distance Davis could see a few lifeboats, rafts, an occasional swimmer. But none was close, and most had already been picked up by the circling destroyers. Davis took off his shoes. He inflated his life jacket, and went down a line into the water. He began to swim.

In Dr. Davis' mind was the same fear that haunts almost everyone on leaving a sinking ship in tropic waters—the fear of sharks. The fact that he was alone intensified the fear. He kept looking behind him. And close behind he saw what appeared to be the nose of a large fish.

Dr. Davis began to swim faster. The nose of the fish followed. In desperation, Davis hit at it. And caught his own wallet! Somehow it had floated out of his pocket and tangled onto his shirttail.

Later, safe aboard one of the circling destroyers, Dr. Davis said that he had been far more afraid of his own wallet than he had been of the ship sinking under him.

Operations were performed at sea under many strange and sometimes wild conditions. But none were wilder than those under which young Dr. George Blankenship, barely out of medical school, once worked.

Dr. Blankenship was the doctor aboard the destroyer *Taussig* when that ship, along with the rest of Admiral Halsey's 3rd Fleet, was caught in a tremendous typhoon. The wind blew with such force that the ships' instruments were ripped away and there was no way to measure the force. Waves ninety feet high crashed upon the ships. Men were washed overboard; three destroyers went down; and 790 men were lost.

It was in the midst of this, just as the storm roared toward its peak, that Dr. Blankenship reached his decision. Carpenter's Mate Laurence Barriere had acute appendicitis. He would have to be operated on immediately. And in this storm there was no possible chance of transferring him to a larger ship.

The sick bay on the *Taussig* was actually the doctor's office, and it was barely large enough for that. The operating table was a board with a two-inch rim around it. In normal weather, this might keep a patient from rolling off, but now the *Taussig* herself threatened to overturn with every roll. It was impossible to stand up without holding on.

The doctor squeezed himself into the narrow space between the bolted-down table and the bulkhead. Now no matter how the ship pitched and rolled, the doctor, the operating table, and the bulkhead all moved together. So did the patient, tied to the table. Chief Pharmacist's Mate Herbert Marsh acted as Blankenship's assistant, clinging to the operating table with one hand and trying to reach for instruments with the other. Pharmacist's Mate 1st Class Claire Dyball was anesthetist. Corpsman Wilton Sharpe's job was to brace himself against the bulkhead and try to hold Dyball and Sharpe upright.

Outside, the storm reached its peak. Around the *Taussig* other ships were going down. On the bridge the captain could not worry about the surgical operation going on below. He could not try to hold the ship steady. He could only fight to keep it afloat.

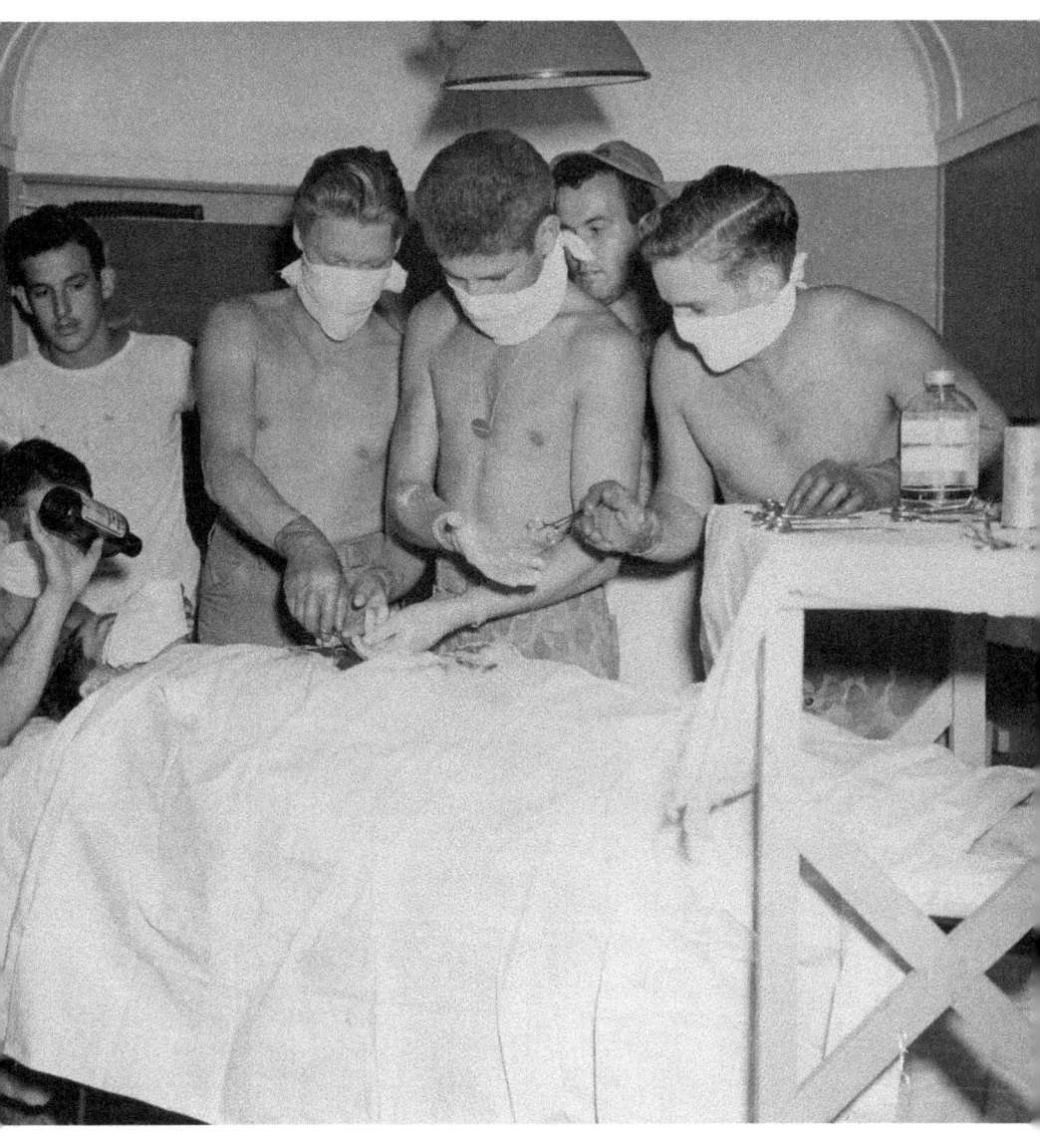

As the anesthetist drips ether into an improvised gauze mask, a young surgeon and his assistants perform emergency surgery somewhere in the South Pacific.

A giant wave caught the *Taussig* and twisted it as if to break the ship in half. Rivets in the deck snapped. Water began to pour through the overhead into the sick bay. Within moments the doctor, corpsmen, and patient were soaking wet. The deck of the sick bay was six inches deep in water. Dr. Blankenship kept working.

After two hours the operation was complete. A rubber sheet was spread over the patient to protect him. The ship moved gradually out of the heart of the storm into slightly calmer seas.

A week later Laurence Barriere was completely recovered. And the men of the *Taussig*, always a proud ship, did not know if they were proudest of Barriere, Dr. Blankenship, or the captain who had saved their ship in the storm.

Both Barriere and Dr. Blankenship were lucky that the doctor was not prone to seasickness. Not all Navy doctors and patients were as lucky.

Nurse Theresa Hayes—the nurse who had once taught Corpsman Evanisky to give injections—was later serving in a hospital on a Pacific island. One of her patients was a boy with a badly cut face. All Ensign Hayes knew about him was that he had been on a ship sunk during a battle.

One day a Navy doctor came and asked to see this patient. The doctor and boy talked briefly. Then, as the doctor was leaving, he stopped to speak to Miss Hayes again.

"That was a poor job done on sewing up that boy's face," he said.

Doctors do not usually criticize one another's work, and Theresa Hayes was surprised. But she had noticed the boy's face many times.

"Yes," she said. "Whoever the doctor was, he did a poor job."

"All right," the doctor said. His voice was suddenly high with anger. But it was anger at himself, not at her. "So I did a poor job! A man can't do his best work when he's on his knees in a lifeboat, being shot at, so seasick he vomits every other minute. But it had to be done then, even if it is a bad job!" The doctor turned away and went out of the hospital. She never saw him again and did not learn his name.

Many sailors, like this doctor, never got over the tendency to be seasick in rough weather. The captain of an aircraft carrier, looking over the report of his medical department, noticed that the term *mal de mer* had been used on a number of occasions. He called in the ship's doctor.

"By *mal de mer* you just mean the man is seasick, don't you?"

"Yes, sir," the doctor said.

"Then why not just write that?"

"Well, sir, I didn't think it sounded good to keep reporting that sailors were seasick."

The captain grinned. There were times when he got seasick himself. "All right," he said. "In the future, if it's an enlisted man, just report him as seasick. If it's an officer, say *mal de mer*. And if it happens to be the ship's captain—well, just say the cause of illness is unknown."

As the war progressed, carriers proved to be among the most effective ships in the Navy. It was natural, therefore, that they were a chief target of the enemy. Loaded with bombs and aviation gasoline, they were highly vulnerable. There was no more awesome sight than a carrier on fire.

Each carrier had at least two doctors—a ship's doctor for the crew and a flight surgeon for the aviators.

Dr. Roy Gunther of Anna Maria, Florida, was one of the doctors picked to work with fliers. Before the war he held a private pilot's license and so already knew something about flying. Also, many of the problems brought on by high-altitude flying can affect the eyes and nose, and Dr. Gunther was an eye, ear, nose, and throat specialist. Even so, after joining the Navy he was given further intensive training. Finally he was sent to join the *Manila Bay*, an escort carrier in the Pacific.

Whenever planes were taking off or landing, the flight surgeon's station was on the open flight deck where he could be ready for any emergency. Wounded men under great nervous tension sometimes had strange reactions. During the Battle for Leyte Gulf a plane crashed on the *Manila Bay*'s deck. The pilot was bleeding badly from a wound in the head. Quickly Gunther climbed onto the plane's wing. He told the pilot not to move; the corpsmen would lift him out and take him below.

"No!" the pilot shouted. "I can walk! I don't want to be put on a stretcher!" He was afraid that it would mean his wound was worse if he had to be carried to sick bay.

Minutes later another plane landed with the pilot shot through the leg. Gunther went to cut open the man's trousers so that he could get at the wound without moving the leg. "Don't do it!" the pilot pleaded. "You'll ruin the trousers."

About a month after the Battle for Leyte Gulf, a young man came on board the *Manila Bay* to serve as ship's doctor. He was just out of medical school and so new in the Navy that the gold braid on his uniform was still shiny. At this time the *Manila Bay* was not in combat and the young doctor complained to Gunther that he had no work to do in the sick bay.

"You're lucky," Gunther told him.

But the young doctor kept complaining.

A few weeks later, on January 4, 1945 the *Manila Bay* was part of a large fleet that was headed for the invasion of Luzon in the Philippines. In the late afternoon they were attacked by Japanese *kamikazes*. One of the suicide planes dived through a storm of antiaircraft fire to strike the *Ommaney Bay,* a carrier close behind the *Manila Bay*. Instantly a tremendous cloud of smoke and flame exploded upward. It was followed by more and more explosions. The *Ommaney Bay* went down, and the *Manila Bay* picked up 126 survivors, many of them wounded.

Now the young doctor had work to do. All the rest of that afternoon and all night, he and Gunther worked together. Bleary-eyed, they finally got a few hours sleep. But the next afternoon they were once more at battle stations—the young ship's doctor in sick bay, Gunther on the flight deck. More Japanese suicide planes were in the area. American fighter planes rose to meet them.

Sixteen of the *kamikazes* broke through the fighters to dive on the ships. From the flight deck Gunther saw planes flash across the sky. The sky itself was almost obscured by bursting clouds of antiaircraft fire. Planes exploded and plunged burning into the sea. But one *kamikaze* crashed into the heavy cruiser *Louisville*. Another hit the cruiser *Australia*.

Gunther was standing beside a friend, one of the ship's officers.

"Good old *Manila Bay*," the officer said. "We've always been a lucky ship. We've never…" And then he screamed, "Look out!"

Gunther whirled, and looked for a split second. The plane was coming directly out of the sun. He saw it only as a dark blur, the bomb hanging beneath it. Then he was running, diving headlong into the radar room. The ship's officer, close beside him, dived into the radio room.

An instant later the plane crashed into the ship. Gunther felt himself lifted and hurled first against a bulkhead, then the deck. He rolled, dazed, but finally stumbled to his feet.

Almost instantly he was knocked down again. Something crashed down on his head. (Later he realized that it was a typewriter; but he was wearing a helmet and the blow only stunned him for a minute.)

Two *kamikazes* had crashed into the *Manila Bay* within seconds of each other. Gasoline hoses were ripped apart

Crewmen fight raging, gasoline-fed fires on the flight deck of the carrier *Saratoga* after being hit by several *kamikazes* off of Iwo Jima. The twisted remains of one of the Saratoga's own planes lie in the center. February 21, 1945

and flames spread across the deck. As the fires spread, the ship's ammunition began to explode.

It was now that the long hours of training paid off. The ship's crew fought the fires. Corpsmen dived into burning compartments to bring out the wounded. Working on the open deck, behind whatever shelter could be found, Gunther and his corpsmen gave emergency first aid. Some casualties were immediately sent below to sick bay; others were bandaged and left on the deck.

The radio room in which Gunther's friend had taken shelter was a mass of smoke and flame. Time and again one corpsman plunged into the room, feeling his way, bringing out anyone he could find. They were all dead. But the corpsman kept going back until his own lungs were seared by smoke and fire. Abruptly he began to have convulsions. Quickly Gunther put an oxygen mask over the corpsman's face. This stopped the convulsions, but they started again when the oxygen was removed. Gunther had been deeply impressed by the boy's heroism; even so, he could not devote all his time to one patient with others lying all around. He told another corpsman to continue giving the oxygen, and turned to the next casualty.

Eventually the fires were put out and all the wounded taken below decks. In the operating room Gunther and the young ship's doctor worked, but not as a team now. There were too many patients for both doctors to care for the same man. They worked through the night—it was the second night in a row—and the next day. Later Roy Gunther could never remember just when or where he slept or when he went back to work. The hours, days, and nights blurred into one another.

Somewhere in this period the young ship's doctor raised his drawn face and looked across the small room at Gunther.

"Roy," he said.

"Yes?"

"If I ever again say another word about not having any work to do, shoot me, will you?"

Meanwhile, the *Manila Bay* limped on with the fleet. The dead were buried at sea, the wounded men finally taken care of. The flight deck was repaired, and the ship stayed in action.

IWO JIMA AND OKINAWA
CHAPTER TEN

Six weeks after the *kamikaze* pilots dived into the *Manila Bay*, and while fighting continued in the Philippines, the U.S. Navy began the invasion of Iwo Jima.

Iwo Jima is a small island only two miles wide and about five miles long. It has no harbor. Before the war it was under Japanese control. Very few people lived there; indeed, around the world very few people had ever heard of Iwo Jima. Certainly young Jim Bradley, going to school in the United States, had never heard of it. But after the spring of 1945 he would never forget it.

Iwo Jima lies about halfway between Guam and Tokyo, approximately 700 miles from each. Early in 1945 the United States needed Iwo as a base for fighter planes to protect the big bombers that flew from Guam to attack Japan. The Japanese desperately needed to hold Iwo. As a result, the tiny island became the scene of one of the bloodiest battles of World War II. The casualties among the Marines who attacked Iwo were extremely high. But the casualties among the corpsmen whose only job was to save life, not destroy it, were higher even than among the fighting men.

The invasion began on the morning of February 19. The day was clear, windy, and cool. The sea was fairly rough. As usual, the big battleships stood well offshore, firing their 16-inch guns over the tops of other ships. Closer to shore were the cruisers, then the destroyers and gunboats, all firing steadily. Through these passed the landing craft carrying the Marines and the Navy corpsmen who went with them. Ahead of them Iwo looked deserted, barren, treeless. The sand of the beach was a volcanic black, and the little island was dominated by an extinct volcano near the southern tip called Mount Suribachi.

From his landing craft Jim Bradley, Pharmacist's Mate 3rd Class, saw the volcano and the flash of Japanese guns along its side. But it was well to the south of him, and he had no way of knowing how events on that dark slope would affect his life.

Bradley, assigned to the 2nd Battalion of the 28th Marines, was in the ninth wave of landing craft. The first wave had gone ashore against comparatively light opposition. The second wave followed close on its heels. But many of the landing craft were wrecked in the high waves that pounded the beach. A few yards back from the water the sand was like black powder. The armored amphibians sank in the loose sand and stalled. Others piled up behind them. The Marines ran past them, sinking ankle deep in the loose sand, but still met by only light gunfire.

The Japanese had deliberately held fire. They had allowed the first waves of Marines to move inland, beyond concrete bunkers hidden beneath the sand. And then the Japanese opened up with every gun on the island. Rifles and machine guns raked the Marines who had gone inland.

Wounded Marines, assisted by hospital corpsmen and less seriously wounded comrades, trudge toward an aid station through Iwo Jima's volcanic sand.

Mortars and artillery poured shells upon the beach, adding to the wreckage.

From his landing craft just offshore Bradley could see his friend. Pharmacist's Mate Clifford Langley, in a boat just ahead of him. Langley's craft hit the beach perhaps ten seconds before Bradley's. Then Bradley was splashing his way through the surf and found Langley already kneeling beside a wounded man giving first aid. Five seconds later and a few yards away Bradley began to treat his first casualty.

An aid station was set up in a shellhole. It was a shallow hole. Bullets and shrapnel ripped into its sides. Shells burst around them. Even so, the hole offered some shelter. But Bradley and the other corpsmen could not stay here. The wounded lay elsewhere and had to be brought to shelter.

Crawling, sometimes racing from one shellhole to another, the corpsmen went to the wounded Marines. Clutching a casualty by the collar, an arm, a leg, each aid man crawled back, dragging a wounded man behind him. And then he went after another wounded Marine.

In the aid stations scattered all along the beach, the doctors gave emergency treatment. In one station Keith Wheeler, a war correspondent, was crouching beside Lieutenant Commander Herbert Eccleston, the battalion surgeon, and Lieutenant John Mortell, the dentist. Suddenly a bullet crashed into Wheeler's jaw, angled downward through his throat and out the other side. It cut both the external and internal jugular veins. Normally he would have bled to death in a few minutes. But Wheeler had scarcely fallen before Dr. Eccleston was probing for the veins, clamping them off. Lieutenant Mortell slipped a needle into his arm and, exposing himself to Japanese fire by doing so, held a plasma bottle so that the life-sustaining fluid could flow into Wheeler's vein, replacing the lost blood. Only half-conscious, Wheeler heard someone say, "This fellow sure picked the right time to get hit—standing beside the two best doctors in the division."

With the next letup in the shelling, litter-bearers carried Wheeler back to the beach. Suddenly the shelling began again. The litter-bearers put the stretcher on the ground, then lay flat around it. Their bodies made a kind of foxhole for the wounded correspondent.

The shelling was still going on when Wheeler heard one of the litter-bearers shouting, "There's a boat! Hey! Hold that boat!" Then the corpsmen were on their feet, carrying the stretcher, struggling across the narrow beach into the surf. The stretcher was passed onto the boat. And the four filthy, exhausted corpsmen turned back once more to the island that Keith Wheeler was so glad to be leaving still alive.

Foot by foot and yard by yard the Marines fought their way inland. They captured an airfield and drove south to the foot of Mount Suribachi. Now the job was to capture the mountain that dominated the island and from which Japanese guns could pour fire on the men below. Pharmacist's Mate Jim Bradley was to accompany the Marines who climbed Suribachi.

The sides of the volcano rose so steeply it would have been hard going under any conditions. But the volcano's sides were also pockmarked by hundreds of caves in which Japanese guns were hidden. Looking up the ragged mountain, Bradley wondered how it would be possible to get wounded Marines down it, and how to get supplies up it. But his job was to go with the first wave of attackers and give first aid. Other corpsmen would have to take the wounded men away, and bring in new supplies for Bradley to use.

Even though this concrete Japanese air-raid shelter has been damaged by an American shell, hospital corpsmen find it useful as a first-aid station on Iwo Jima.

Offshore Navy ships pounded the sides of the volcano with a terrific barrage. Shells of all sizes tore into the mountain as though to rip it apart. Gradually the barrage climbed higher up the slope. As it did the Marines surged upward after it, Bradley with them.

It was slow, fierce going, a few yards at a time. For three days the Marines fought their way upward. Casualties were high. Bradley had no idea how many men he treated, giving emergency treatment, praying that what he did was right: morphine to deaden the pain, plasma to keep them alive. For three days litter-bearers, working under Corpsman Ralph Gillespie, took the wounded back down the steep slope of the mountain, and brought supplies back up it.

"Never in all the time I was on Suribachi," Bradley said later, "did I run out of supplies. I don't know how the litter-bearers managed it. We hadn't cleaned out the Japs completely, and every time those fellows went up or down the mountain it was like running a gauntlet of Japanese fire."

On the morning of February 23 the Marines reached the crest of the mountain. From somewhere a man produced a flag and thrust the staff into the ground. But it was a small flag. It could not be seen at a distance. Later in the morning someone brought a larger flag, and six Americans raised it while still under Japanese fire. Five of them were Marines. The sixth was Corpsman James Bradley. But he thought little about it at the time and minutes later was taking care of more wounded Marines.

With Suribachi secure, the Marines turned toward the north end of the island. By March 12, Bradley was the only corpsman with the 2nd Battalion who had not been wounded. Ralph Gillespie, who had done such heroic work on Suribachi, had lost a leg. Bradley began to feel that he led a charmed life.

And then he was shot through both legs.

Bradley did not know who gave him first aid. He was in shock. But gradually, as he became conscious, he had the impression that he was back in the United States in training. "Only this time," he said later, "it was my turn to be in the litter."

At the aid station which Bradley had left only a short time before. Dr. James Wittmier, his own battalion surgeon, dressed his wound. Then once more he was being carried, this time to a slightly more secure field hospital. Here some of the shell fragments were taken from his legs. The next morning he was on a plane for Guam and a Navy hospital. From Guam he was sent to Hawaii, from Hawaii back to Oakland, California. Here he was assigned to Ward 4A—the very same ward where he had done his first duty after finishing his corpsman training.

It was in this hospital, almost well again, that he suddenly found himself surrounded by doctors, nurses, public-relations officers, and newspapermen.

"Why," everybody kept shouting, "didn't you tell us you were in the picture?"

"What picture?" Bradley asked.

"The one of raising the flag on Suribachi!"

"I don't know what you're talking about," Bradley said. "I was on Suribachi. But if there was any picture taken, I don't know anything about it."

They showed him the picture then. A newspaper

Six marines raise the second American flag on Mount Suribachi. Until 2016 it was believed that the second Marine in front, from the right, was Corpsman James Bradley. It's now known this was Private First Class Franklin Sousley and that Bradley did not help raise the flag.

photographer named Joe Rosenthal had taken a picture of the six Americans raising the flag on top of the volcano. Very quickly it had become the most famous picture of the war. Later it would win a Pulitzer Prize, be reproduced on a U.S. stamp and as a bronze monument to the Marine Corps.

Because he had been in the picture, Bradley was flown to Washington. He met President Truman; he met the Secretary of the Treasury and the Navy's Surgeon General. Then he was sent on a tour of the country to sell war bonds. He made speeches from coast to coast.

"I think I was more afraid making speeches," Bradley said later, "than I was on Suribachi."

The fighting on Iwo Jima had scarcely ended before the United States launched a new and even greater invasion, this time against the island of Okinawa. Okinawa was a much larger island than Iwo, and even closer to Japan. With Okinawa in American hands, the United States would be set to invade Japan itself if necessary. Both sides knew this, and both sides threw everything possible into the battle. During the fierce fighting both Navy corpsmen (serving with the Marines) and Army medics won the Congressional Medal of Honor. The stories of two of them —Robert Bush and Desmond Doss—are very different in detail, but each illustrates the aid man's true heroism and devotion to duty.

Robert Bush was barely fifteen years old and going to

high school in Menlo, Washington, when the war started. He watched the growing number of men and older boys in uniform, and felt very left out. When he was seventeen he could stand it no longer. He quit school and joined the Navy. He became a corpsman and was assigned to the 2nd Battalion of the 1st Marine Division. He was with them on May 2, 1945 when the battalion was ordered to move against a heavily defended Japanese position on Okinawa.

This was a country of low, rugged hills, pock-marked with caves. Here and there was an occasional, flat-topped tree that looked strangely like the trees in Japanese paintings. By the time the 2nd Battalion started up the hill, artillery fire had blasted the tops from the trees. Only the torn trunks were left, looking like driftwood skeletons among the rocks and caves.

Slowly the Marines moved upward. Robert Bush went with them. He carried two heavy first-aid kits, and strapped to his thigh was a pistol. This pistol marked a change from the early days of the war when all corpsmen went unarmed. Because the Japanese seemed to consider it more important to kill one corpsman than a dozen Marines, many of the corpsmen in the Pacific began to carry either pistols or carbines for self-defense. Robert Bush carried a pistol.

From the crest of the hill the Japanese fired mortars, machine guns, and rifles. As the Marines pushed closer, the Japanese threw hand grenades down the slope. The grenades bounced from rock to rock before they exploded.

Casualties were heavy. Later Robert Bush's citation would read that he "constantly and unhesitatingly moved from one casualty to another to attend the wounded Marines falling under the enemy's murderous barrages." Time and again he dragged a man down the slope to a place of safety, then climbed up the hill again.

The Marines reached the top of the hill. As they pushed over the ridge Lieutenant James Roach, Bush's platoon leader, was hit and fell. Moments later the aid man was beside him.

It was a ghastly wound, but one thing Bush had learned was never to give up hope. Kneeling beside the lieutenant, Bush cut away part of the uniform. He poured sulfa powder into the wound to prevent infection and applied a battle dressing. But already Roach had lost a great deal of blood and was going into shock. The corpsman prepared a plasma bottle, slipped the needle into Roach's arm, and kneeling beside the wounded man held the bottle high so that the plasma would drain into his vein.

Suddenly the Japanese staged a counterattack. With a great shout of *"Banzai!"* they rushed from caves and pillboxes. The Marines were driven back. Staggering, many of them wounded, they reeled past the spot where the corpsman knelt beside the wounded lieutenant. Bush stayed where he was. The Japanese surged toward him, bayonets fixed, guns firing.

A bullet struck Bush, knocking him over; but he held to the plasma bottle with his left hand. With his right he drew his pistol and fired at the oncoming Japanese. A grenade fragment struck his head, destroying one eye. He dropped the plasma bottle now. His pistol was empty. He threw it aside, picked up a carbine someone had abandoned, and opened fire. Before it was empty he had killed six Japanese, one within a few feet of himself. And the Marines who had momentarily reeled backward were attacking again. They drove the Japanese from the crest of the hill.

Robert Bush dropped the empty carbine. He went back and knelt beside the lieutenant. Wiping the blood from his eyes with one hand, he groped for the plasma bottle with the other. Later his Medal of Honor citation would say:

"With the hostile force finally routed, he calmly disregarded his own critical condition to complete his mission, valiantly refusing medical treatment for himself until his officer patient had been evacuated, and collapsing only after attempting to walk to the battle aid station."

Happily, both Bush and Lieutenant Roach lived.

Robert Bush undoubtedly saved his own life and that of Lieutenant Roach by the use of weapons as well as medical knowledge. On the other hand, Desmond Doss, from Lynchburg, Virginia, absolutely refused even to touch a gun under any circumstances. Because of this refusal he was, for a time, the laughingstock of his Army outfit. He was called a coward. He was threatened with court martial and prison. But he became one of his country's greatest heroes.

It is a strange story.

Desmond Doss belonged to the Seventh-Day Adventist Church. This church recognizes Saturday as the Sabbath, and its members are forbidden to do any work on the Sabbath. Also, its members do not believe in killing, even in a war. Therefore they refuse to serve as armed soldiers. On the other hand, as patriotic Americans they are completely willing to serve as unarmed medics and risk their own lives to save others.

A thin, shy, quiet man, Desmond Doss was deeply religious. On his first night in the Army he knelt beside his cot to say his prayers as he had always done. Some of the other soldiers howled with laughter. Some threw shoes at him. They began to make fun of him and call him "Holy Joe."

Moreover, Doss refused to work on Saturday. He was willing to work with the patients on this day, but not to go on training marches or stand K.P. duty. Most medics were given basic military training, but Doss simply refused to touch a gun of any kind. He would have been court-martialed, but the leaders of his church obtained a statement signed by President Roosevelt saying that, as a conscientious objector, Doss did not have to carry a weapon. He kept this paper with him throughout the war.

Doss began to earn the respect of his fellow soldiers on their first long training march. It was twenty-five miles, under a broiling summer sun. Some men passed out from the heat. Some fell out with blistered feet. When a man fainted, Doss was quickly beside him to help. Then he ran to catch up with the others. When men began to limp,

Doss bandaged their blistered feet, and did not worry about his own. He did not look strong, but he was wiry and tougher than anyone suspected.

Doss' outfit saw its first combat in the invasion of Guam in July 1944. Still green, frightened, the troops were moving through thick trees when a sudden burst of machine-gun fire cut down one of the men. The others took cover. But Doss, his first-aid kits flapping at his sides, raced to the fallen man. The man was dead, and there was nothing Doss could do. But his fellow soldiers began to look at him with new respect.

The respect turned into deep affection in the days that followed. Whenever patrols were sent forward, Doss went with them. He could have stayed behind and waited until there was a call for help. But the men felt better if there was a medic close by. Everyone knew that a few minutes could mean life or death to a wounded man.

After Guam, with only a brief rest, Doss' outfit was sent to the Philippines. Here he continued to go on patrols, even after the medical officer told him not to. The men needed him, Doss said.

Many of the men were not religious. And yet they found it strangely comforting to know that Desmond Doss prayed for all of them. Often men who could not pray themselves asked Doss to pray for them.

Two of Doss' fellow medics were killed on Leyte. Each time Doss risked his life to go to the fallen man, even though in vain. Doss himself seemed to have a charmed life. Once he went after a soldier who had been wounded

Native Okinawans escorted to safety by a Marine. 1945

in a rice paddy. Other soldiers watching through field glasses from a hillside saw a Japanese sniper hidden in the paddy. The sniper kept his rifle trained on Doss. But he never fired. No one could say why. Doss reached the wounded man and brought him back to safety.

After the Philippines were secure, Doss' outfit was sent to take part in the invasion of the island of Okinawa. And it was here that the story of Desmond Doss became a legend known to all the Army.

A line of rugged hills crossed the southern end of Okinawa. Near the center was a sharp cliff about thirty feet high, the Maeda Escarpment. This was the key to the defense of the whole of the southern end of the island, and the Japanese had fortified it heavily. Doss' company was given the job of scaling this cliff and attacking the gun emplacements beyond.

Under cover of darkness a few men climbed the cliff. Doss was one of them because in mountain training at home he had been good with ropes and knots. From the top of the cliff the men lowered rope ladders so that others could climb up.

The first attack was to be made by a small squad of picked men. Very few of them expected to come back alive. They asked Doss to pray for them. He did. Then, with Doss at their heels, they crawled toward the Japanese pillboxes. The men destroyed a half-dozen Japanese fortifications without one of their group being killed or wounded. But the attack by another American company to one side failed. Caught in a crossfire, Doss' group was forced back over the cliff—still without a casualty.

This luck did not hold. The battle for the cliff continued, day after day, night after night. The men had little or no sleep. Time after time Doss climbed the cliff and went forward to aid wounded men. The nights were almost more dangerous than the days. At night, both Japanese and Americans shot at anything that moved. But whenever a call came for a medic, Doss answered. By now his uniform was not only filthy—it was almost a solid mass of dried blood.

One night Doss was trying to get some sleep in a cave along with his lieutenant and five riflemen. Suddenly the Japanese began to throw grenades at the mouth of the cave. All the Americans dashed out, Doss the last one. In the darkness he fell over the edge of a ravine. His leg was so badly bruised that he could barely walk. But by now one medic had been killed, another wounded. Doss was the only medic left in his company. He stayed.

Then it was May 5, 1945—a Saturday. In the early morning Doss sat with his back against the foot of the cliff reading his Bible. His captain stopped by. He explained that his company had been ordered to attack in force.

"You don't have to go with us, Doss," he said. "But the men would like to have you."

"I'll go," Doss said. "But wait until I finish my Sabbath lesson."

And so the attack waited. Doss finished his prayer, put his Bible in his pocket, and the men of Company B began their attack. They went up the rope ladders that hung down the face of the cliff and moved across the ragged, shell-torn land toward the Japanese fortifications.

The Japanese had ordered a large-scale counterattack for this same time. Suddenly a terrific barrage of artillery and mortar fire struck the advancing Americans. From every Japanese pillbox machine guns opened fire. And from behind the barrage Japanese troops charged forward. The American advance stopped. The men reeled backward. The retreat turned into a rout. Men raced for the edge of the cliff to tumble down it to comparative safety. Within minutes Desmond Doss and the wounded were the only Americans left on the escarpment.

There were wounded men everywhere. They lay sprawled in front of Doss and to right and left. Artillery and mortar shells burst in one continuous explosion among them.

Through the bursting shells Doss crawled to the nearest man. There was no time for first aid. He caught the man by the collar and pulled him back to the edge of the cliff. There was a rope here—and Doss was good with ropes and knots. He tied two loops in the rope, slipped one over each leg of the wounded man, tied another loop around his chest, and lowered him over the edge of the cliff.

At the foot of the cliff, soldiers lifted the wounded man out of the loops. Doss pulled the rope up. He crawled to another wounded man, dragged him back, and lowered him over the edge. Then another. And another. He did not count. Nobody counted. Shells were falling. Men already wounded were being killed. Doss kept working. He did not even have time to wonder why the Japanese advance had stopped. But it did, perhaps because of counter fire from American artillery in the rear.

When it was over no one knew with certainty how many American soldiers Desmond Doss had saved that day. Doss' commanding officer said it was one hundred.

Doss shook his head. "I don't think it was more than fifty, Captain."

"We'll split the difference," the captain said. "I'll make an official report that it was seventy-five."

Desmond T. Doss, the first conscientious objector to receive the Congressional Medal of Honor. Okinawa, May 1945

After the war the American Government would erect two monuments at the edge of the cliff. One in English, one in Japanese, they read:

PFC. DESMOND T. DOSS

This Seventh-Day Adventist medical aid man of the 77th Infantry Division received the Congressional Medal of Honor for valor during the battle for the Maeda Escarpment. Pfc. Doss remained on top of the escarpment after his unit was driven off, searched for the wounded men, carried 75 of them to the edge of the cliff and lowered them over the side in a rope litter.

But the battle for the Maeda Escarpment did not end the war. After an American counterattack captured the escarpment, the men pushed on. On the night of May 21 Doss was on night patrol with his company. In the darkness the men became separated. Doss was in a foxhole with two other soldiers when suddenly a Japanese grenade landed among them. Almost without thinking, Doss put his left foot on the grenade and pushed it into the soft earth.

The explosion lifted him into the air. He could remember seeming to spin, then nothing. When he regained consciousness, he felt his leg. It was still there, but his trousers were soaked with fresh blood from hip to foot. The two men who had been in the foxhole with him were gone. Doss began to crawl back toward the American lines, but fainted.

It was daylight when litter-bearers found him. They put Doss on a stretcher and started for the rear. But when they passed a man bleeding from a head wound, Doss ordered the bearers to put him down and take the other soldier instead.

The litter-bearers were Doss' friends. "Your leg is in bad shape," they told him. "We are taking you in."

"No," Doss said. "We've been told to get men with head wounds first."

Reluctantly, the litter-bearers put Doss down and took up the other soldier. Soon Lewis Brooks, a friend of Doss' from his own company, came by. He was wounded, but only slightly, and could walk. "Come on," he told Doss. "I'll help you."

And still it was not over. The men moved slowly, painfully. Brooks with one arm around Doss' waist. Doss with an arm around Brooks' neck. Neither of them heard the sniper's rifle. The bullet hit Doss' arm where it curved around Brooks' neck. It shattered the bone below the elbow, went through the forearm, and smashed into his arm just above the elbow. The two men stumbled into a shellhole and lay flat. Here Doss, with Brooks' help, put a crude bandage on his own arm. He tried to bandage some of the seventeen wounds in his left leg. And then he passed out once again.

This time when he regained consciousness he was in a hospital. Eventually he would recover. And Lewis Brooks would say, "If it hadn't been for Desmond's arm around my neck, the bullet that hit him would have killed me."

So even to the last Desmond Doss had carried out the job of the U.S. military doctors and aid men: to save the lives of others, even at the risk of their own.

Desmond Doss on top of the Maeda Escarpment, Okinawa. May 4, 1945.

AUTHOR'S NOTE

Doctors are, proverbially, the busiest of people with the least time for personal matters. So I would particularly like to thank all those who have taken time to write me letters, or to sit down and talk about their war experiences. There is not space to list them all here, but thanks.

My thanks also to the former corpsmen, medics, and nurses who have furnished me with stories, general background information, and helped check for errors. And to one of the truly great heroes of the war, Desmond Doss, my deep appreciation for permission to retell his story. Most of the information used here is from the very good book about him, *The Unlikeliest Hero*, written by Booton Herndon and published by Pacific Press.

Then there are those unsung heroes and heroines of almost any book of nonfiction: the librarians and information services who knock themselves out to help a writer even though he is unknown to them. So I would particularly like to say thanks to the librarians of Bradenton, Florida, public library; the Sarasota, Florida, public library; the Manatee Junior College library; to the officers and men of the Magazine and Book Branch of the Defense Department's Directorate of Information; and especially to Esther Rohlader of the Historical Unit, the Walter Reed Army Medical Center.

Many thanks.

WYATT BLASSINGAME
1969

ABOUT THE AUTHOR

Wyatt Blassingame wrote 600 magazine articles and short stories, five adult novels, and almost 60 books for young readers over a writing career that lasted longer than a half-century. A keen and curious observer of life and natural history, he wrote about the egrets, raccoons, crows, and other creatures that showed up in his backyard on the island of Anna Maria, Florida. He studied and wrote about sharks, snakes, turtles, armadillos, and even wrote a book on *The Little Killers: Fleas, Ticks, Mosquitos*. While everything interested him, he became known as a Florida writer, as many of his novels and stories were set there.

Born in Alabama, Wyatt graduated from the University of Alabama in 1929. Wyatt had many adventures as a young man. During the Great Depression, he earned the nickname "Hobo" for his skill at jumping trains and hitchhiking across the country to find work. He was a police reporter and taught college journalism before moving to New York City where he began writing mystery and detective stories for the "pulp" magazines, earning a penny a word. In one year, he pounded out 500 stories on his Underwood typewriter. He enlisted at the outbreak of World War II and served in the Navy in the Pacific, earning a Bronze Star. His experiences led him later to write about those he saw as true heroes and heroines, those who served on the medical front.

In 1936, he married Gertie Olsen and moved to Anna Maria Island, Florida, an idyllic slice of white sand in the Gulf of Mexico, where they raised two daughters. Wyatt continued writing until his death in 1985, filling his free time with fishing, swimming, and gardening. He kept nature notes of the Island's weather, tides, plants, and animals, and for his novels, he researched the Florida cattle industry, the real estate boom of the 1920s, and the history and culture of the Seminoles. In 1952, he was asked to write a book for young readers about a subject dear to his heart: *The*

Great Trains of the World. That book was followed by dozens more, including *Frogmen in World War II, The French Foreign Legion, The Incas and the Spanish Conquest,* and *The Look-It-Up Book of Presidents,* which has remained in print, updated every four years. He wrote biographies of Eleanor Roosevelt, Sacagawea, and Thor Heyerdahl, among others. Wyatt also published a series of Tall Tales about mythic and legendary characters, like Paul Bunyan and Pecos Bill.

Wyatt Blassingame was a man with foresight and compassion. He and his wife were early advocates for the environment, ahead of their time. They served on Anna Maria's city planning and zoning boards, and both fought to prevent opening Tampa Bay to oil exploration. Wyatt was also an early defender of civil rights. His prize-winning story, "Man's Courage," dealt with racial hatred in the Army, and won the Ben Franklin Award for the Best Short Story of 1956.

With his bushy eyebrows and deep southern drawl, Wyatt Blassingame was respected by his friends and circle of fellow writers, and beloved by his family. His daughter Peggy gave him five grandchildren and ten great-grandchildren, and his daughter April's four children blessed him with nine more grandchildren, all of whom will be able to read this story again in print, thanks to Purple House Press. The family and descendants of Wyatt Blassingame are happy and grateful that his work is available to a new generation.

KATHI DIAMANT
Granddaughter of Wyatt Blassingame
October 2021

www.ingramcontent.com/pod-product-compliance
Lightning Source LLC
Chambersburg PA
CBHW041324110526
44592CB00021B/2814